easy food for
utter indulgence

easy food for
utter indulgence

the ultimate in comfort food, with over 50 delectable recipes for
breakfasts, brunches, teatimes and suppers

maxine clark
photography by martin brigdale

To my marvellous Mum

This edition is published by Aquamarine

Aquamarine is an imprint of Anness Publishing Ltd
Hermes House, 88–89 Blackfriars Road, London SE1 8HA
tel. 020 7401 2077; fax 020 7633 9499
www.aquamarinebooks.com; info@anness.com

© Anness Publishing Ltd 2001, 2005

UK agent: The Manning Partnership Ltd
6 The Old Dairy, Melcombe Road, Bath BA2 3LR
tel. 01225 478444; fax 01225 478440; sales@manning-partnership.co.uk

UK distributor: Grantham Book Services Ltd
Isaac Newton Way, Alma Park Industrial Estate, Grantham, Lincs NG31 9SD
tel. 01476 541080; fax 01476 541061; orders@gbs.tbs-ltd.co.uk

North American agent/distributor: National Book Network
4501 Forbes Boulevard, Suite 200, Lanham, MD 20706
tel. 301 459 3366; fax 301 429 5746; www.nbnbooks.com

Australian agent/distributor: Pan Macmillan Australia
Level 18, St Martins Tower, 31 Market St, Sydney, NSW 2000
tel. 1300 135 113; fax 1300 135 103; customer.service@macmillan.com.au

New Zealand agent/distributor: David Bateman Ltd
30 Tarndale Grove, Off Bush Road, Albany, Auckland
tel. (09) 415 7664; fax (09) 415 8892

A CIP catalogue record for this book is available from the British Library.

Publisher Joanna Lorenz
Managing editor Linda Fraser
Design Manager Clare Reynolds
Senior editor Margaret Malone
Designer Mark Latter
Food stylist Linda Tubby
Stylist Helen Trent
Copy editors Susannah Tee and Jenni Fleetwood
Editorial reader Jonathan Marshall
Production controller Ann Childers

Previously published as *Comfort Food*

10 9 8 7 6 5 4 3 2 1

Notes

Bracketed terms are intended for American readers.

For all recipes, quantities are given in both metric and imperial measures
and, where appropriate, measures are also given in standard cups and spoons.
Follow one set, but not a mixture, because they are not interchangeable.

Standard spoon and cup measures are level.
1 tsp = 5ml, 1 tbsp = 15ml, 1 cup = 250ml/8fl oz

Australian standard tablespoons are 20ml. Australian readers should use
3 tsp in place of 1 tbsp for measuring small quantities of flour, salt, etc.

Medium (US large) eggs are always used unless otherwise stated.

The very young, the elderly, pregnant women and those in ill-health or with
a compromised immune system are advised against consuming raw eggs or
dishes and drinks containing raw eggs.

contents

in the
comfort zone

The phrase "comfort food" conjures up many things. It can be a lazy lie-in in a sunlit bedroom with a bacon sandwich and a cup of tea or coffee, it may involve lounging on the sofa on a rainy afternoon, watching an old movie and eating your way through a home-made pizza, or it may be sharing a hot buttered scone with strawberry jam and clotted cream with a friend. Whatever makes you feel good – that's comfort food. It lifts the spirits; warms you when you're cold and revives you when you're weary. It can be a reward, a remembrance of good times past, or simply an excuse to indulge.

When I was asked to write this book, it seemed like a dream come true – but choosing precisely what to include proved surprisingly tricky. Everyone I spoke to had different ideas of exactly what constituted true comfort food. There were some constants – apple pie and roast dinners among them – but in the end the list inevitably had to be subjective and so the recipes featured here are my idea of what comfort food is.

I grew up in Scotland, so there are definite echoes of my childhood in this collection. For instance, I just had to include porridge – so very warming and fortifying on a chilly Highland morning – as well as the pancakes my grandmother used to make for me after school. Real, rich shortbread was another item on my personal list of must-haves,

to be absolutely comfortable, **eat where your mood takes you**

most of all, these are hands-on recipes, and the pages of the book should be stained with use – a sign of success

along with cullen skink, a wonderfully creamy concoction of soft leek and smoked haddock soup, which we often ate as children.

Nostalgia is inevitable when the conversation turns to comfort food, and a few nursery staples such as fish pie seemed to strike a chord with

all. However, comfort food and drinks can – and should – also include the contemporary. In fact, as I worked on this book, I realised that a number of old favourites really only remained so because I had adapted them over the years. A classic dish such as a bread and butter pudding has been transformed into a superbly rich hazelnut and pain au chocolat pudding, for example.

Another feature of the recipes was the presence of excellent ingredients from around the world. Most people's palates are quite sophisticated these days, and unusual foodstuffs are increasingly easy to find, so its not necessary to stay in the nursery to get the "oooh!" factor. Just thinking about the range of pasta and rice, the huge selection of vegetables, herbs and spices, oils, vinegars and breads that are now on offer, makes my head spin. These ingredients bring alive old classics, enhancing flavours and delighting in differing textures.

European, American, Australian, Thai – comfort food knows no boundaries. One of my favourite treats is French rarebit with sweet shallot and garlic confit, which was inspired by a skiing holiday where I became pleasantly sidetracked and spent more time visiting the skilled cheesemakers of Gruyère than speeding down the slopes.

This brings me to the essence of all comfort food. Whether international or local, a familiar old classic or a recent creation, truly comforting dishes are always home-made. This is because they are as enjoyable to plan and prepare as they are to eat. Taking pleasure in the ingredients, equipment, cooking and serving are all part of the comfort. Some equipment and ingredients simply invite you to use them, especially if you know that they themselves have been made with care (such as my Gruyère cheese). There's also something very reassuring about being in your own kitchen, handling

utensils you've grown to cherish, such as a well-seasoned pancake pan or a really good wok, or setting out favourite coffee cups alongside the

I will drink coffee out of a mug, but it tastes better in my big cup and saucer at home

coffee pot and the freshly-made scones and jam on a tray given you by a friend. Sometimes just the planning, shopping and buying, preparation and serving is extremely comforting, and the eating a wonderful bonus.

Nothing in this book is too difficult or pretentious. The recipes can be eaten alone, or combined with others. Some are suitable for large numbers of people; while others are single servings, but can be multiplied to suit the occasion. One or two are best cooked ahead for eating next day, so that flavours have a chance to mature, and some can be cooked and kept in the refrigerator to provide emergency comfort stocks.

There are several delicious drinks in this book, including a hot toddy, mulled wine, hot buttered rum and egg nog. All slide seamlessly into the comfort category, the alcohol contributing to their warmth. Drinks are

comfort food is not rushed and half-hearted, but made with **care, anticipation** and a **dash of creativity**

eminently transportable, which is another important criterion for comfort food. It's essential to be able to enjoy a snack or meal wherever you are relaxing, be that the bedroom, living room or kitchen table. If hunger strikes when you're sprawled on the rug playing a board game, or sitting on the sofa immersed in the television, it makes sense to prepare food

and drink you can enjoy just where you are. With the exception of some heartier dishes designed for sharing with family and friends at the table, all the recipes here are intended for easy eating.

To cook and be cooked for, are among the most precious things we experience in life. I hope this book helps that happen. **Maxine Clark**

breakfast in bed

Eating breakfast in bed is my idea of utter heaven. Some may disagree, citing squashed crumbs and spilt drinks, but what's a little mess? Bed just spells comfort. We rest, play, recover from illness, forget our troubles, and keep snug and cosy there. The bed has a womb-like association with safety and warmth – it's where we often feel most happy and truly relaxed.

The best breakfast in bed is brought to you, thus avoiding any interruption of idleness. I can't think of anyone who doesn't like snuggling down under the covers while wonderful smells emerge from the kitchen, and someone else

this is the **time to spoil yourself** with something
a little more **exotic** than cereal

rattles the cups. However, there's also a distinct decadence in making your own favourite food and taking it back to bed, with papers and magazines piled high. This is the time to spoil yourself with dishes that take a little more time to prepare than a bowl of cereal and are made with extra special ingredients:

larger, richer duck's eggs instead of hen's; the best dry cure bacon or pancetta; creamy, buttery hollandaise sauce – and even a little caviar for decoration. A decent tray is a must, with high sides to prevent things sliding about, and a cloth is a nice touch. My mother always put a cloth embroidered with little cockerels on the tray when she brought us meals when we were ill in bed. Use a cherished teapot that is too special for everyday use, coffee bowls too big for rushed workday breakfasts and pour milk into a jug (pitcher). Warm everything, too: the plates, cups, bowls and teapot.

An electric juicer is ideal for rustling up simple fruit juice mixes, and I also have a favourite frying pan for cooking breakfast things. It is heavy, made from iron and blackened with use and age, and it goes into the oven, handle and all.

The recipes included here are my idea of soothing, satisfying and utterly self-indulgent eating. Most of them are quick and easy, but be prepared to linger a little. Some of life's pleasures shouldn't be rushed. If you

can't face cooking first thing in the morning, but still want something substantial, try a smoothie. This is a good summer choice but, when rain batters the windowpanes, you can't beat a big bowl of hot porridge. Standing in the kitchen stirring porridge is therapeutic in itself, and the combination of creamy porridge and velvety, rich, spiced plums is a wonderful wake-up call. The bacon sandwich and classic eggs bénédict are both Saturday breakfast treats that will relieve any hangover, if made just right. It always amazes me that it is possible to make such sublime dishes from a few simple, good quality ingredients. Then, there's the ultimate way of preparing croissants – overflowing with softly scrambled eggs and caviar.

Remember, breakfast in bed is not a hurried affair, rather there's a certain thrill about taking the time to cook a meal and prepare the tray just as you wish. Any effort spent in preparing the meal can only add to the pleasure of eating your breakfast in the comfort of your own bed.

the best
breakfast
in bed is the
one that is
**brought
to you**

The secret of the smoothie was revealed to me by an Aussie friend – always serve them ice-cold. Whizzing them up with ice is the perfect way to ensure this. I keep an ice tray of frozen orange juice at the ready – and it's a great way to add extra flavour.

honey and banana smoothie
marbled with hot chocolate sauce

First make the hot chocolate sauce. Break up the chocolate and put the pieces into a bowl placed over a pan of barely simmering water. Leave undisturbed for 10 minutes until the chocolate has completely melted, then add the water, syrup and butter and stir until smooth. Keep warm over the hot water while you make the smoothie.

Place all the smoothie ingredients in a blender or food processor and blend until smooth. Pour into big, tall glasses, then pour in some chocolate sauce from a height. This cools the thin stream of sauce slightly on the way down, so that it thickens on contact with the cold smoothie. The sauce swirls around the glass to give a marbled effect, which is very theatrical and sure to impress first thing in the morning.

serves 2 generously

450g/1lb/2 cups mashed
ripe banana
200ml/7fl oz/scant 1 cup natural
(plain) yogurt
30ml/2 tbsp mild honey
350ml/12fl oz/1½ cups orange juice
ice cubes, crushed

For the hot chocolate sauce
175g/6oz plain (semisweet)
chocolate with more than 60%
cocoa solids
60ml/4 tbsp water
15ml/1 tbsp golden
(light corn) syrup
15g/½oz/1 tbsp butter

On cold days there is nothing better than a bowl of warm porridge. Whether to add salt or sugar is completely up to you – Scottish highlanders used to eat it with cream and honey. The extremely grown-up plums make the porridge extra special.

real porridge with plums

To make the poached plums, pour the wine into a pan and stir in the sugar. Add the cinnamon stick and the star anise. Bring to the boil and boil for about 1 minute.

Halve and stone (pit) the plums. Add the plums to the wine syrup and barely simmer for about 10 minutes until just beginning to soften. Allow the plums to cool in the liquid while you make the porridge. Pour 1 litre/1¾ pints/4 cups water into a pan and bring to the boil. Tip in the oatmeal, stirring to prevent lumps from forming. Turn down the heat and simmer for 10–15 minutes, or until the porridge is as thick as you like it. Season with salt to taste. Try eating porridge in the traditional way. Pour it into deep, warmed bowls and serve the plums alongside, with really cold cream in a separate bowl. Take a spoonful of porridge and dip it into the cream. Eat this, then take a spoonful of plums. Savour the contrast – this is not a dish to be hurried.

serves 4

300ml/½ pint/1¼ cups fruity red wine
75g/3oz/scant ½ cup caster (superfine) sugar
1 cinnamon stick
1 star anise
450g/1lb red or purple plums
115g/4oz/1 cup medium oatmeal
salt
single (light) or double (heavy) cream, to serve

This is a particular favourite of mine, first encountered when I was a student at Leith's School of Food and Wine. It was one of the recipes we had to be able to cook quickly. There were a lot of curdled hollandaises and burnt muffins in the beginning but, with practice, we mastered it. I still love it today.

eggs bénédict

Bring a medium pan of water almost to the boil. Crack each egg into a cup and slide it into the water. Poach the eggs, allowing the water to just tremble but not boil, for 1 minute.

Remove the pan from the heat and allow the eggs to sit for 10 minutes by which time they will be perfectly cooked.

Meanwhile, grill (broil) the bacon or pancetta until crisp. Keep it warm. Toast the muffins and butter generously; keep warm.

Make the quick hollandaise. Season the egg yolks with salt and pepper, beat well and put into a food processor. If you only have a large food processor, you could use a "stick" blender or even an electric hand beater – just remember to use a deep jug (pitcher) or small basin to mix it in, as the quantity is quite small. Put the lemon juice and vinegar into a small pan and heat until it boils. With the processor (blender or beater) running, immediately pour the hot liquid on to the eggs.

Melt the butter until it is foaming. Again, with the machine or beater running, pour the boiling hot butter on to the eggs in a steady stream. (The butter will thicken the egg yolks like a warm mayonnaise.) Add the tarragon. Thin the hollandaise down by beating in a little warm water.

Lift the poached eggs out of the water with a slotted spoon and drain on kitchen paper. Sit a toasted muffin on a warm plate, top with crisp bacon and place an egg on top. Spoon the hollandaise over the top and eat immediately.

serves 2

2 large (US extra large) free-range
(farm-fresh) eggs, chilled
4 Ayrshire bacon rashers
or unsmoked rolled pancetta
(the circular shape fits the
muffin perfectly)
2 English muffins or crumpets
butter

For the quick hollandaise
2 large free-range (farm-fresh) egg
yolks, beaten
10ml/2 tsp lemon juice
10ml/2 tsp tarragon wine vinegar
115g/4oz/½ cup butter
15ml/1 tbsp chopped
fresh tarragon
salt and ground black pepper

The secret of making the perfect bacon sandwich is to use all your favourite ingredients. For instance, if you love back bacon, then use it, though thin crisp bacon is just as good – I'd recommend grilling it rather than frying, but for how long is up to you. Use toast or a soft morning roll. Toast should be crisp on the outside and soft in the middle and buttered with softened butter. As to sauce, my preference is tomato, and it has to be Heinz, but some swear by brown sauce. Whatever you do, eat this sandwich hot.

simply the best
bacon sandwich

Make a pot of tea and let it brew (to my mind, this is not an optional extra, but an essential companion to a bacon sandwich). Grill (broil) the bacon rashers to your liking, then put on a dinner plate, cover, and keep them warm on the floor of the grill (broiler). While the bacon is grilling, gently warm a bread roll, if using, underneath the grill pan.

If toasting the bread, don't use a toaster, use the grill instead as you will get a better, more even result. Toast the bread after you have grilled the bacon, using the same grill pan to add some extra flavour. Butter both pieces of the bread or toast, or split and butter the roll.

Top the bread or toast with the bacon, or fill the roll. Add the sauce and top with the remaining slice of bread or toast. Lightly press down and cut in half with a serrated knife. Pour a cup of tea and eat the sandwich immediately.

makes 1

4 best bacon rashers (strips),
dry-cured if possible
a large, soft morning roll or 2 thick
slices fresh white, crusty bread
softened butter
sauce of your choice, such as
tomato or brown sauce
a pot of tea, to serve

we've all had one of those
terrible hangovers
– and this is the **perfect cure** with a lovely big
mug of tea

serves 4

4 large slices of country (preferably
sourdough) bread
75g/3oz/6 tbsp butter, plus extra
melted butter
3 shallots, finely chopped
2 garlic cloves, finely chopped
675g/1½lb field (portabello) or
chestnut mushrooms, thickly sliced
75ml/5 tbsp dry white wine
45ml/3 tbsp chopped fresh parsley
salt and ground black pepper

Everybody loves garlic mushrooms. I thought it would be fun to make them a little
more sophisticated, and use big, juicy flat mushrooms instead of bland buttons. I've
added some wine to deepen the flavour even further (a decadent touch first thing in
the morning), and heaped the robust mushrooms on griddled chewy country bread.

garlic mushrooms on bruschetta

Toast the bread on both sides on a hot ridged griddle. This will give the bread a striped
charred effect as if done on a barbecue. Real bruschetta is grilled over glowing coals and
takes on the smoky flavour of the burning charcoal. The ridged griddle must be heated until
very hot, though, or the bread will take ages to colour and will just dry out. If you don't
have a griddle, toast the bread under a hot grill (broiler) on both sides until quite dark.
Brush the toasted bread with the extra melted butter and keep warm.

Melt the butter in a frying pan, add the shallots and garlic, and cook for 5 minutes until
golden. Add the mushrooms and toss well. Fry over a high heat for 1 minute. Pour over the
wine and season well. Keep the heat high and cook until the wine evaporates. Lightly stir in
the parsley. Pile the mushrooms on to the bruschetta and serve immediately.

This is one of the most comforting, self-indulgent dishes I know. Lox is the Jewish word for smoked salmon, and this recipe is a real Jewish deli classic. A few basics: be generous with the smoked salmon; use loads of the best cream cheese you can find (no low-fat versions please!); and always warm the bagels.

bagels and lox with cream cheese

Preheat the oven to 200°C/400°F/Gas 6. Put the bagels on a large baking sheet and warm them in the oven for 4–5 minutes.

Remove the bagels from the oven, split them in two and spread with cream cheese. Pile the salmon on top of the bagels and grind over plenty of black pepper. Squeeze over some lemon juice, then top with the other bagel half and eat while still warm. For an easy and elegant touch, place a wedge of lemon in the centre of a small square of muslin (cheesecloth), bring up the edges to enclose it, tie with fine string and put it on the plate. The lemon can now be squeezed without fear of a pip shooting into your eye.

serves 2

2 bagels
115–175g/4–6oz/½–¾ cup full-fat
cream cheese
150g/5oz sliced best
smoked salmon
ground black pepper
lemon wedges, to serve

A classic combination that relies on very fresh eggs and very buttery croissants. Crème fraîche adds a little bite while the pancetta contributes a crunchy smokiness.

croissants with scrambled eggs, caviar and frazzled pancetta

Preheat the oven to 200°C/400°F/Gas 6. Place the croissants on a baking tray and warm them in the oven for about 5 minutes, then switch the oven off.

Melt the butter in a non-stick frying pan until foaming, then add the pancetta or bacon. Cook over a high heat until very crisp. Lift out on to a plate and keep warm in the oven with the croissants. Leave the butter and fat in the pan and reheat gently.

Lightly beat the eggs with the crème fraîche and season with salt and pepper. Split the croissants in half and place on warmed plates. Pour the eggs into the pan and stir with a wooden spoon. Cook over a low heat, stirring slowly, until the mixture is creamy and thick. Remove the pan from the heat.

Fill the croissants with the scrambled eggs, spoon over the caviar and lay the pancetta on top. Be a little adventurous with the presentation – it makes all the difference, especially when

the ingredients are so special. It is said that we eat with the eyes first, then the mouth. Setting the bacon so that it points skywards gives the whole thing a distinctly cheeky look, and an extra spoonful of real caviar on the side looks truly decadent – keep the jar handy for seconds. Sprinkle with chopped chives and serve immediately.

serves 4

4 croissants
50g/2oz/¼ cup butter
12 thin smoked pancetta or
streaky (fatty) bacon
rashers (strips)
8 free-range (farm-fresh) eggs,
at room temperature
60ml/4 tbsp crème fraîche
60ml/4 tbsp Avruga or Keta caviar
45ml/3 tbsp chopped fresh chives
salt and ground black pepper

it's **never too early** to indulge
in a little caviar

Sicilians fill large brioches with ice cream and eat them on their way to work. I've never had the courage to do this in broad daylight, but it's definitely worth trying at home alone or with someone who won't mind the mess. The hot fudge sauce is added for sheer indulgence.

sicilian brioche breakfast
with hot fudge sauce

Set the oven to 200°C/400°F/Gas 6 and, while it is heating, make the hot fudge sauce. Break up the chocolate and put the pieces into a bowl placed over a pan of barely simmering water. Leave undisturbed for about 10 minutes until the chocolate is completely melted, then stir in the butter.

Add 75ml/5 tbsp boiling water to the chocolate and butter, stir well to blend, then stir in the syrup, sugar and vanilla essence. Pour and scrape into a pan and bring to the boil, then turn down the heat and allow to barely bubble for 5 minutes.

Meanwhile, put the brioches on a baking sheet and warm them in the oven for 5 minutes. Herein lies the secret to this dish: warm the brioches so that they are slightly crisp on the outside but soft, fluffy and warm on the inside.

After 5 minutes, remove the pan of sauce from the heat. Immediately split the brioches open and gently pull out a little of the insides. Generously fill each brioche base with ice cream and gently press on the tops. Put into serving bowls or on to plates and pour over the hot fudge sauce. Serve immediately. (Any leftover fudge sauce can be stored in a jar in the refrigerator to melt at a moment's notice.)

serves 2

2 individual brioches
2 huge scoops of best vanilla or
coffee ice cream

For the hot fudge sauce
50g/2oz best dark (bittersweet)
chocolate with 70% cocoa solids
15g/½oz/1 tbsp butter
30ml/2 tbsp golden
(light corn) syrup
150g/5oz/scant 1 cup soft light
brown sugar, sifted
5ml/1 tsp vanilla essence (extract)

from the tray

Temptation on a tray – that's what this chapter is all about. The sort of food you fancy when it's raining and you're stuck indoors, working at the computer, doing household chores or sharing a pot of tea or cup of coffee and something nice to eat with friends. The accent is on food that's easy to eat and impossible to ignore. A tray signals teatime but it could be from a trolley too, though, sadly, the welcoming rattle of a loaded trolley coming towards you is a rarely heard sound these days.

The custom of serving food at teatime is still one that I find particularly irresistible. I was lucky enough to have two grandmothers and a mother who all

loved baking, so their tins were always full (as we say in Scotland). While it can be quite difficult to find the time, home-baked goods are in a class of their own – so completely different to those bought ready-made. I recently moved house, and, amid towers of packing cases, was able to offer a new neighbour a thick slice of dark, sticky gingerbread, made three days earlier and brought with me for some

licking your **sticky fingers** prolongs the pleasure

much needed comfort and sustenance during the move. If you can bear to leave this cake undisturbed in the tin for at least two days, it really does live up to its name. It also keeps for ages (though not if I can help it). Another great choice to have in the tin is my rich carrot cake topped with mascarpone icing. I've added chopped pineapple to the basic recipe to make it even moister, and the longer you can leave the cake, the better it will be.

American muffins are a must in a book of comfort food. They can be mixed in minutes, and the smell drives you crazy as they bake. Add chopped-up butterscotch or toffee to the mixture and it melts to make deliciously rich, gooey pockets. As for scones, another must-have, I went on a hunt for the perfect English scone recipe and feel very content with the version eventually arrived at here.

Scotch pancakes simply had to be included, too. The best recipe I know comes from my Grandmother Tootie. As youngsters, my sister and I would devour these divine little treats, smothered in butter, in front of the electric fire while watching children's television, all the while keeping one eye on the open hatch to see when the next batch would be ready.

in a few moments the bubbles appear and you know the pancakes are ready to flip over – wait another eternal minute and they are ready to eat

Sweet bakes aren't the only items to take from the tray. There are also big sandwiches. Not dainty little triangles, but great towers of taste and texture. Some, such as the steak sandwich with basil aioli, take a little longer to prepare, but the basic components can be made ahead of time and kept in the refrigerator. A classic egg mayo sandwich is another good choice. Deceptively simple, this must be made with the best ingredients.

Eating off the tray is "digging in" food – something to interrupt work for, as well as satisfy hunger. It is food eaten in the hands with a napkin, and is invariably deliciously messy.

I have always loved buttered scones with jam. Ever since I first tasted real Cornish cream teas on holiday, the contrast of warm, buttery scone, home-made jam bursting with fruit, and thick clotted cream has been etched on my memory, periodically emerging as a desperate craving in times of stress.

proper soda scones
with jam

Preheat the oven to 230°C/450°F/Gas 8. Sift the flour, salt and baking powder, if using, into a mixing bowl. Rub in the butter until the mixture resembles fine breadcrumbs.

Whisk the lemon juice into the milk and leave for about 1 minute to thicken slightly, then pour into the flour mixture and mix quickly to form a soft but manageable dough. I have found that the wetter the mixture the lighter the resulting scone will be, but if too wet they will spread out, amoeba-like, while baking in the oven.

Knead the dough lightly to form a ball, then roll it out on a floured surface to a thickness of at least 2.5cm/1in. Using a 5cm/2in biscuit cutter and dipping it into flour each time, stamp out 12 scones, and place them on a well-floured baking sheet. Re-roll any trimmings and cut out more if you can.

Brush the tops of the scones lightly with a little milk and then bake them for about 20 minutes, or until risen and golden brown. Remove the tray from the oven and wrap the scones in a clean dishtowel to keep them warm and soft until ready to serve. Eat with your favourite fruit jam and a generous dollop of cream.

makes about 12

450g/1lb/4 cups self-raising
(self-rising) flour or 450g/1lb/
4 cups plain (all-purpose) flour and
10ml/2 tsp baking powder
5ml/1 tsp salt
50g/2oz/¼ cup butter, chilled and
cut into cubes
15ml/1 tbsp lemon juice
about 400ml/14fl oz/1⅔ cups milk,
plus extra to glaze
fruit jam and clotted cream, or
double (heavy) cream, to serve

This is my Grandmother Tootie's recipe for pancakes. We often dropped in to her house on the way home from school and she would stand over the griddle making pancake after pancake, almost as fast as we could eat them. Spread them with softened butter so that it melts into the pancakes a little before you eat them.

tootie's pancakes

Sift the flour with the bicarbonate of soda, cream of tartar and salt into a mixing bowl. Stir in the sugar. Make a well in the centre and pour in the beaten eggs. In a separate bowl, mix the lemon juice with the milk and leave to thicken slightly.

Add half the soured milk to the flour mixture and, using a whisk, gradually draw the flour into the liquid, whisking well to break up any lumps. Now add the rest of the milk, little by little, until the mixture is slightly thicker than double (heavy) cream. If you have time, leave the mixture to stand in a cool place for 30 minutes. This is not absolutely necessary but it will make the pancakes lighter.

Heat a griddle or heavy frying pan until medium hot. Lightly grease with a little butter. Drop large spoonfuls of batter, spaced well apart, on to the griddle or fying pan. In a few moments the pancakes will set and small bubbles will appear all over the surface. At this stage turn each pancake over to cook on the other side for a minute or so. Lift the cooked pancakes out of the griddle or pan and put them on to a plate covered with a dishtowel to keep warm while you make the others. The pancakes shouldn't cook too quickly, so adjust the heat as you go. Eat while still warm, with plenty of butter. A little fruit jam, too, would not go amiss.

serves 2

300g/11oz/2⅔ cups plain (all-purpose) flour
5ml/1 tsp bicarbonate of soda (baking soda)
5ml/1 tsp cream of tartar
pinch of salt
75g/3oz/6 tbsp caster (superfine) sugar
2 eggs, lightly beaten
5ml/1 tsp lemon juice
about 400ml/14fl oz/1⅔ cups milk
butter, for greasing and serving

the best thing about making pancakes
is listening to the gentle hiss of the batter
as it drops on to the hot griddle

Lining a muffin pan with paper cases takes all the frustration out of struggling with muffins that insist on sticking to the pan. Make up the two mixtures the night before and stir them together first thing next day for an irresistible mid-morning treat. Instead of butterscotch, try adding chocolate chips, marshmallows or blueberries.

gooey butterscotch **nut muffins**

Preheat the oven to 200°C/400°F/Gas 6. Line a 9–12 cup muffin pan with paper cases or grease with butter. With floured fingers, break the butterscotch sweets into small chunks. Toss them in a little flour, if necessary, to prevent them from sticking together.

Sift together the flour, sugar, baking powder and salt into a mixing bowl. Whisk together the egg, milk and oil or melted butter, then stir the mixture into the dry ingredients with the sweets and nuts. Only lightly stir together as there should still be a few lumps of flour in the mixture.

Spoon the mixture evenly into the prepared muffin pan, filling the paper cases about half full. Bake for 20 minutes until well risen and golden brown. Cool in the pan for 5 minutes, then remove and transfer the muffins to a cooling rack. As with all quick breads, these are best eaten the same day.

Try spreading these with a Spanish treat called *dulce de leche* (available in larger supermarkets); it is rather like condensed milk that has been boiled in the can until caramelized – a favourite in my younger days. Drizzle over and eat.

makes 9–12

150g/5oz butterscotch
sweets (candies)
225g/8oz/2 cups plain
(all purpose) flour
90g/3½oz/7 tbsp golden caster
(superfine) sugar
10ml/2 tsp baking powder
2.5ml/½ tsp salt
1 large (US extra large) egg, beaten
150ml/¼ pint/⅔ cup milk
50ml/2fl oz/¼ cup sunflower oil or
melted butter
75g/3oz/¾ cup chopped hazelnuts
butter for greasing, if needed

Not just a tough piece of dry beef stuffed into an undercooked baguette, this is the real thing. Thick-cut sirloin steak is marinated and chargrilled, then sliced thinly and piled on to a toasted ciabatta loaf that has been generously spread with a rich basil and garlic aioli. To top it off, a heap of caramelized onions. Irresistible.

the ultimate steak sandwich
with basil aioli and caramelized onions

serves 4

400g/14oz beef sirloin, cut as one piece
30ml/2 tbsp teriyaki marinade
5ml/1 tsp sesame oil
black olive or sun-dried tomato ciabatta loaves, split in half (or any similar bread with character)
olive oil, for brushing
75g/3oz bag fresh salad leaves

For the basil aioli
175ml/6fl oz/³⁄₄ cup light and fruity olive oil
115g/4oz/2 cups fresh basil leaves
2 large garlic cloves, crushed
1 egg yolk
fresh lemon juice
salt and ground black pepper

For the caramelized onions
50g/2oz/¹⁄₄ cup unsalted (sweet) butter
2 large onions, finely sliced
10ml/2 tsp caster (superfine) sugar
15ml/1 tbsp balsamic vinegar

Trim any fat or sinew from the beef and place the beef in a china or glass dish. Liberally spoon the marinade and oil over the meat, coating it well. Cover and leave to marinate, preferably overnight or for at least 4 hours in the refrigerator, turning occasionally.

Make the aioli up to 2 hours before serving. Put the olive oil and basil in a blender or food processor and process until really smooth. Pour into a jug (pitcher). Add the garlic, egg yolk and a pinch of salt to the blender or food processor (don't worry about cleaning it first as it all goes into the same jug) and process until very smooth. With the motor running, very slowly pour in half the basil oil, in a thin steady stream, until the mixture starts to thicken. Stop the machine and scrape down the sides. Add a squeeze of lemon juice, start the machine again, then continue to pour in the oil more boldly until it has all been added and the aioli is quite thick. Check the seasoning – it should be bursting with garlic. Set the aioli aside in the refrigerator, to ensure it does not separate.

A little while before you are ready to make the sandwich, caramelize the onions. Melt the butter in a frying pan. Add the onions and stir to coat well. Add 30ml/2 tbsp water, cover and cook over a gentle heat for 10 minutes. Uncover, sprinkle with the caster sugar and balsamic vinegar and turn up the heat. Cook over a brisk heat for 10 minutes more, stirring from time to time, and watching the mixture constantly. The onions should start to turn a beautiful rich brown colour. Set aside when cooked.

Heat a ridged griddle pan until smoking hot. Remove the meat from the marinade and pat dry with kitchen paper. Sear the meat on the griddle for 2–3 minutes on each side, then reduce the heat to medium and cook the meat, without moving, for another 4 minutes. Turn it over and cook for 4 minutes more. Lift on to a plate, cover with foil and leave for 10 minutes to allow the meat to relax. This cooking time produces medium rare meat, which is ideal, but if you like your meat well done, cook for a little longer.

Split the ciabatta loaves and brush with olive oil, then toast on the griddle or under the grill (broiler). Wrap in foil to keep warm while you slice the beef thinly.

Spread one half of the bread liberally with the basil aioli, top with the beef, then the onions, more aioli and finally the ciabatta top. Cut the sandwich in two or four and eat immediately, accompanied by the salad leaves.

just **thinking** about this recipe **conjures up** the sweet
smell of onions **caramelizing** in a pan, the
juicy steak waiting its turn

There's something about the mix of chicken and avocado that is very comforting. Mango, too, has that pleasing, luscious taste and texture and, when combined with oak-smoked chicken and creamy avocado, the taste buds really tingle.

toasted baguette with smoked chicken and mango avocado salsa

Preheat the oven to 200°C/400°F/Gas 6. Pull out some of the inside of each baguette half and brush the halves with melted butter. Place, cut-side uppermost, on a baking tray and bake for about 15 minutes. Remove from the oven, cover with foil and keep warm.

Meanwhile, make the salsa. Cut two mango slices, one from each side of the stone. Peel, chop the flesh and place in a bowl.

Halve, remove the stone and peel the avocados, then roughly chop and stir into the mango. Add the lime juice, coriander and chilli seasoning and stir well. Taste and season with salt and black pepper. (If possible, make the salsa a little ahead of time, so that the flavours can develop.) Generously spoon the salsa into the hollowed baguettes and top with the sliced smoked chicken. Mix the yogurt with the smoked paprika, salt and pepper, and spoon over the chicken. Sprinkle with chopped chives. Eat immediately.

serves 2

2 short baguettes, split lengthways
75g/3oz/6 tbsp butter, melted
1 smoked chicken, meat removed and sliced
300ml/½ pint/1¼ cups natural (plain) yogurt
2.5ml/½ tsp *pimentón dulce* (smoked Spanish paprika)
60ml/4 tbsp chopped fresh chives
salt and ground black pepper

For the salsa
2 medium, ripe mangoes
2 ripe Hass avocados
juice of 1 lime
45ml/3 tbsp chopped fresh coriander (cilantro)
5ml/1 tsp mild chilli seasoning

eating this is a two-handed job, the pleasure being in the contrast of soft, spicy filling with the crunch of the crust

This may be simple enough to make, but to get it right demands careful preparation and good quality ingredients. When the egg is perfectly hard-boiled, the mayonnaise freshly made and the bread soft and crusty, this is one of the most satisfying sandwiches to eat. Mustard and cress is traditional, but you can use watercress, rocket or, in fact, any salad leaf that is vaguely peppery. I go even further, and add chopped spring onions and dill-pickled cucumber.

classic egg mayo sandwich
with mustard and cress

First make the mayonnaise. It really isn't that difficult. Just remember that all the ingredients should be at room temperature to ensure the mixture doesn't curdle. Beat the egg yolks with the mustard and salt in a small bowl. Add a tablespoon of oil, then, using an electric whisk or a balloon whisk (though using this will give you a serious arm-ache), whisk until the mixture begins to thicken. Add another spoonful and whisk well again until thickened. Repeat this process until you've used half the oil. Beat well, then add the vinegar or lemon juice and beat again. Now add the rest of the oil in a thin, steady stream, beating all the time, until all the oil is added and the mayonnaise is nice and thick. Taste and add salt and pepper to taste. (At this stage you can flavour the mayonnaise with ingredients such as curry paste or powder, herbs, spices, mustard or wasabi paste.) Cover and store in the refrigerator until needed.

To hard-boil the eggs perfectly, place them in a pan and cover with cold water. Bring the water to simmering point, then simmer for exactly 7 minutes. Immediately pour off the boiling water, set the pan in the sink and fill with cold water. Keep the water running into the pan for a couple of minutes to cool the eggs down quickly, then turn it off and let the eggs sit in the cold water for 3–4 minutes. Lift them out of the water, tap each one to crack the shell and peel. Place each egg back in the water to keep it fresh, while you finish peeling the rest.

Roughly chop the eggs and place in a bowl. Add the chopped spring onions and dill-pickled cucumber and enough mayonnaise to make a thick, spreadable mixture. Taste and adjust the seasoning.

Butter one side of each slice of bread. Liberally scatter some cress, watercress or rocket over the butter on two of the slices and pile the filling on top. Cover with more leaves and lightly press the two remaining slices of bread on top. Cut the sandwiches in two with a serrated knife and they are ready to eat.

serves 2

4 free-range (farm-fresh) eggs
4 spring onions (scallions), chopped
I fat dill-pickled cucumber, roughly chopped
softened butter
4 thick slices bread, freshly cut from a crusty multigrain or malted grain loaf
mustard and cress, watercress, or rocket (arugula)
salt and ground black pepper

For the mayonnaise
2 free-range (farm-fresh) egg yolks
2.5ml/½ tsp Dijon or English (hot) mustard
300ml/½ pint/1¼ cups mild olive oil
15ml/1 tbsp white wine vinegar or a squeeze of lemon juice
salt and ground black pepper

Universally loved, this is one of the most irresistible cakes there is.
Everyone has their own version; I've added poppyseeds for colour
and crunch, and pineapple to give it extra moistness. Instead of the
traditional cream cheese icing, I've used Italian marscarpone, which
spreads like a dream and doesn't feel so cloying.

poppyseed pineapple carrot cake with orange mascarpone icing

makes 1 large loaf

250g/9oz/2¼ cups plain
(all-purpose) flour
10ml/2 tsp baking powder
5ml/1 tsp bicarbonate of soda
(baking soda)
2.5ml/½ tsp salt
5ml/1 tsp ground cinnamon
45ml/3 tbsp poppyseeds
225g/8oz/1⅓ cups soft
light brown sugar
3 eggs, beaten
finely grated rind of 1 orange
225g/8oz raw carrots, grated
75g/3oz/⅓ cup fresh or canned
pineapple, drained and
finely chopped
75g/3oz/¾ cup walnut pieces
115g/4oz/½ cup butter,
melted and cooled

For the mascarpone icing
150g/5oz/scant 1 cup mascarpone
30ml/2 tbsp icing (confectioners')
sugar, sifted
finely grated rind of 1 orange

Preheat the oven to 180°C/350°F/Gas 4. Line the base of a
1.5 litre/2½ pint/6¼ cup loaf pan with baking parchment. Grease
the sides of the pan and dust with flour.

Sift together the flour, baking powder, bicarbonate of soda,
salt and cinnamon into a bowl. Stir in the poppyseeds.

Mix together the sugar, eggs and orange rind in a separate
bowl. Lightly squeeze the excess moisture from the grated carrots
and stir the carrots into the egg mixture with the pineapple and
walnut pieces. Gradually stir the sifted flour mixture into the
egg mixture until well combined, then gently fold in the butter.
Spoon the mixture into the prepared pan, level the top and bake
for about 1–1¼ hours until risen and golden brown. (To check if
the cake really is cooked in the centre, push a thin metal skewer
right down into the middle of the cake. Pull it out immediately
and feel if there is any sticky mixture clinging to the skewer. If it
comes out clean the cake is done, if not, pop it back for a further
10 minutes and test again.) Remove the cake from the loaf pan
and allow to cool on a wire rack. Remove the baking parchment
when completely cold.

To make the icing, beat the mascarpone with the icing sugar
and orange rind. Cover and chill until needed. When ready to
serve, beat well, then spread thickly over the top of the cake. Cut
into slices and eat.

This is my favourite gingerbread. The secret of its dark, rich stickiness lies in the huge amount of treacle used. It cries out to be smothered in cool yellow butter or swirls of cream cheese, which are in complete contrast to the cake's taste and texture. It is very tactile and literally sticks to the roof of your mouth when you eat it.

really **sticky gingerbread**

Preheat the oven to 160°C/325°F/Gas 3. Grease and line the base of an 18cm/7in square cake pan that measures about 7.5cm/3in deep.

Sift the flour, ground ginger, mixed spice and salt together into a bowl. Add the ginger and toss it in the flour to coat thoroughly.

Cream the butter and sugar together until fluffy, then gradually beat in the treacle or molasses. Gradually beat in the eggs, then the flour mixture. Dissolve the bicarbonate of soda in the milk and gradually beat this into the mixture. Pour the mixture into the prepared pan and bake for 45 minutes. Reduce the oven temperature to 150°C/300°F/ Gas 2 and bake for a further 30 minutes. The gingerbread should look very dark and slightly risen. The only way to make sure it is cooked is to insert a metal skewer into the middle. If it comes out clean the cake is done. Don't worry if the gingerbread sinks slightly in the middle – it always does. Cool the gingerbread for 5 minutes in the pan, then turn out and cool completely on a wire rack. At this stage, the gingerbread will be dark, but not sticky at all. Keep it for two to three days in an airtight container and the outside will become wonderfully sticky and moist. When ready, slice the gingerbread, spread with butter or cream cheese, and eat.

makes an 18cm/7in square cake

225g/8oz/2 cups plain
(all-purpose) flour
10ml/2 tsp ground ginger
5ml/1 tsp mixed (apple pie) spice
a pinch of salt
2 pieces stem (preserved) ginger,
drained and chopped
115g/4oz/½ cup butter, softened
115g/4oz/⅔ cup dark
muscovado (molasses) sugar, sifted
275g/10oz/scant 1 cup black treacle
or molasses, at room temperature
2 eggs, beaten
2.5ml/½ tsp bicarbonate of soda
(baking soda)
30ml/2 tbsp milk, warmed
butter or cream cheese, to serve

the **longer the cake** is stored in the tin the **better it gets**
— if you can wait that is

on the rug

Lounging on a rug by an open fire is so enjoyable it's almost therapeutic. Whether playing board games, reading a book or doing homework, this is a true comfort zone. It is a place where you can really relax, and is made even more special if there is something to eat and drink that suits the moment. Food that is easily rustled up from yummy ingredients, and can be eaten simply, is the order of the day.

no-fuss food you can eat with your fingers

Toast, in all its guises, is the classic snack for eating on the rug – perfect for adults and children alike. Crunchy on the outside and soft within, it can't be beaten. But good toast is not so easy to make. You need a white crusty loaf that isn't too fresh and doughy, a good serrated knife and a dependable grill (broiler). Cut thick slices of bread – if they are too thin the toast will be hard and chewy, or just shatter and you'll have to start all over again. When both sides are just the right colour, prop the slices against the bread board to steam for 30 seconds before spreading them with softened butter or adding a topping. Just think of sardines on toast, toast soldiers with a boiled egg or crunchy toast fingers topped with warm smoked fish pâté. A personal favourite is cinnamon toast, which I haven't given a recipe for because it's so simple, but it really can't go unmentioned. Here's what you do: toast crustless bread, spread with butter, top with a sprinkling of ground cinnamon and brown sugar, and put under the grill for a few minutes before eating. Delicious with a cup of real hot chocolate.

This chapter includes two wonderful grown-up toast treats. The first is my French rarebit, a mixture of melted Gruyère cheese with mustard, wine and cayenne pepper on crusty bread, served with a sweet shallot and garlic confit.

The second is crunchy finger toasts spread with a peppery smoked mackerel brandade. Both are ideal for enjoying on a wet afternoon.

Eating on the rug is what most children do well, but they can also help to make treats, such as rocky road chocolate bars, and it's a marvellous way of showing them that good things don't have to come out of a packet, as well as teaching them cooking skills for later life. They'll need no encouragement to do the hands-on stuff such as mixing the marshmallows into the melted chocolate or rolling churros in sugar, in preparation for serving.

this is the sort of food that **children will want** to help make

Adult-only drinks such as creamy egg nog and aromatic mulled red wine with port can round off an afternoon on the rug very nicely indeed. To accompany, try oven-roasted nuts, which make a wonderful, spicy snack or, if you prefer something a bit sweeter, individual creamy custard tarts are extremely moreish. Home-made shortbread with its buttery centre and crunchy, sugary crust is delicious with a cup of tea or dipped into a mug of hot chocolate. All of these are just right for some serious afternoon relaxing on the rug.

The inspiration for this recipe came from a skiing holiday in Switzerland when I ate pots of cheese fondue and raclette (melted cheese). If you can imagine grilled fondue on toast, then this is it.

french rarebit with sweet shallot and garlic confit

To make the confit, heat the oil in a large pan over a medium heat. Add the shallots, sliced onions and garlic, stirring to coat with the oil. (My preference is for smoked garlic. It's difficult to get, but the lovely smoky and nutty flavour really comes through the sweetness of the confit to add an earthiness to the whole dish.) Add just a couple of tablespoons of water and put on the lid. Cook slowly for 20 minutes, without lifting the lid, to steam and soften the onions.

Uncover the pan, stir well and continue to cook very slowly for about 1 hour until the onions are very soft and caramelized.

Stir the vinegar and cassis into the pan and season with salt and pepper. Cook for about 10 minutes more, to evaporate the vinegar. The confit should look thick and sticky. Leave to cool, then carefully spoon into a preserving jar, cover with a layer of olive oil and keep in the refrigerator.

To make the rarebit, preheat the grill (broiler). Put the butter, mustard, white wine, cheese and cayenne pepper in a small pan and slowly melt over a gentle heat. Set aside for a moment.

Toast the slices of baguette on one side. Beat the egg yolk into the melted cheese and spread over the un-toasted side of the bread.

Put under the grill for 2–3 minutes until browned and bubbling. Serve with a good dollop of the sweet onion and garlic confit.

serves 4

25g/1oz/2 tbsp butter
5ml/1 tsp Dijon mustard
30ml/2 tbsp medium to sweet white wine
75g/3oz Gruyère or raclette cheese, grated
pinch of cayenne pepper
2 long thick slices crusty French baguette, cut on the slant
2 egg yolks

For the confit
75ml/5 tbsp olive oil
675g/1½lb shallots, quartered
675g/1½lb red onions, finely sliced
4 garlic cloves, thinly sliced (preferably smoked garlic)
120ml/4fl oz/½ cup sherry vinegar or half dry sherry and half balsamic vinegar
30ml/2 tbsp crème de cassis
salt and ground black pepper

One of my favourite dishes is French *brandade de morue*. This is a warm potato, salt cod, olive oil and garlic purée, and is supremely soothing. The right kind of salt cod is often difficult to find outside of France, so I have made a similar dish using smoked mackerel, which gives it a lovely peppery flavour.

brandade of smoked mackerel with crunchy finger toasts

serves 6

450g/1lb peppered smoked mackerel fillets, with skin on
225ml/7½fl oz/scant 1 cup milk
225ml/7½fl oz/scant 1 cup water
sprig of fresh thyme
1 bay leaf
450g/1lb floury potatoes, peeled
150ml/¼ pint/⅔ cup half olive and half sunflower oil
15ml/1 tbsp horseradish sauce
30ml/2 tbsp wholegrain mustard
45ml/3 tbsp chopped fresh parsley
15ml/1 tbsp chopped fresh tarragon
ground black pepper
extra virgin olive oil, for serving

For the finger toasts
6 slices day-old, good white bread
115g/4oz/½ cup butter, melted

First make the finger toasts. Preheat the oven to 180°C/350°F/ Gas 4. Cut the crusts off the bread and brush both sides of each slice with butter. Cut each slice into four fingers and spread out on a baking sheet. Bake for 15–20 minutes until golden brown and crisp. Keep warm.

To make the brandade, place the smoked mackerel fillets in a large pan with the milk and water, thyme and bay leaf. Bring almost to the boil, then remove the pan from the heat and allow the fillets to cool in the liquid.

Meanwhile, in a separate pan, boil the potatoes for about 20 minutes until tender, then mash well. Keep warm. Strain the liquid from the mackerel and reserve. Remove the skin from the fish and flake the flesh.

Heat the oils in a pan until a piece of day-old bread sizzles when added. Add a spoonful of fish and beat well. Keep adding the fish, spoonful by spoonful, over a medium heat, beating until it has all been added. Use a deep pan and an electric beater on slow speed. Be careful to avoid splashes, but once two large spoonfuls have been added there should be no problem. Stir in the horseradish, mustard and herbs, then beat in the mashed potato. Beat in enough of the reserved cooking liquid to give a smooth, creamy consistency, suitable for spreading. Season well with ground black pepper. Pile into a dish and drizzle with a little olive oil before serving warm with the crunchy finger toasts.

I like to serve this drink on the eve of special occasions such as Christmas or Thanksgiving, when all the preparations and planning are done. Its warm, aromatic qualities always make me instantly relax, slow down and enjoy the moment. Freshly roasted nuts are the ideal accompaniment, and can be made beforehand.

mulled red wine with ruby port

Bruise the ginger by lightly hitting with a rolling pin, then place, along with the spices, into a stainless steel or enamel pan and cover with 600ml/1 pint/2½ cups water. Bring slowly to the boil, then boil rapidly for 10 minutes until the liquid is reduced to 300ml/½ pint/1¼ cups. Remove the pan from the heat.

Mix the wine and port together in a jug (pitcher). Line a sieve with kitchen paper, then strain the spiced reduction into the jug containing the wine and port. Rinse out the pan well.

Return the wine and port mixture to the pan and reheat. Put a silver spoon into each warmed glass – this will diffuse the heat and stop the glass cracking – pour in the mulled wine and serve.

makes 1 litre/
1¾ pints/4 cups

15g/½oz fresh root ginger
1 cinnamon stick
4 whole cloves
1 star anise
6 allspice berries, crushed
600ml/1 pint/2½ cups fruity red wine
150ml/¼ pint/⅔ cup ruby port

make a huge amount of these roasted nuts and keep them in an airtight container – you won't regret it

spicy oven-roasted nuts

makes about
450g/1lb

40g/1½oz/3 tbsp butter
15ml/1 tbsp garam masala
450g/1lb mixed skinned nuts, such as almonds, brazils and hazelnuts
5ml/1 tsp salt

Preheat the oven to 150°C/300°F/Gas 2. Melt the butter in a roasting pan and stir in the garam masala, then add the nuts and stir until well coated. Roast for 30 minutes to 1 hour until the nuts are golden, stirring from time to time.

Remove the nuts from the oven and toss them lightly with the salt. Allow to cool completely, then store for at least a day before eating. They will keep in an airtight container for two weeks.

Churros are long, golden doughnuts, which are deep-fried and rolled in caster sugar while still hot. I've had a passion for them since my first encounter with them, bought from a street stall one chilly Easter in Spain. The crunchiness of the sugary crust, the soft inside, and that just-fried smell is irresistible.

real hot chocolate with churros

To make the churros, sift the flour on to a small sheet of baking parchment. Bring the water and milk to the boil in a pan. Tip in the flour and beat vigorously with a wooden spoon, stirring until the dough forms a ball and no longer sticks to the sides of the pan. Remove the pan from the heat and let the dough cool a little. Gradually beat in the eggs, adding just enough to give a piping consistency. Spoon the mixture into a piping bag fitted with a large fluted nozzle.

Preheat the oven to 150°C/300°F/Gas 2. To cook the churros, heat the oil in a deep-fat fryer or wok until a piece of dough sizzles as soon as it hits the oil. Squeeze the piping bag over the pan, snipping off 10cm/4in lengths with kitchen scissors. Fry the churros in batches of 4–6 until golden, then remove them with a slotted spoon, and drain on kitchen paper. Place on a baking tray and keep warm in the oven while making the hot chocolate.

To make the hot chocolate, break up the chocolate and put in a heatproof bowl set over (not in) a pan of barely simmering water. Leave alone for 10 minutes until the chocolate has melted completely. This is the essence of real hot chocolate – it doesn't come as powder in a packet; it is made with the best chocolate you can afford, which is melted and whisked into hot milk – it is how the Spanish and Mexicans have been making it for centuries, and it's ambrosial!

serves 2

115g/4oz plain (semisweet) chocolate with more than 60% cocoa solids
400ml/14fl oz/1⅔ cups milk

For the churros
200g/7oz/1¾ cups plain (all-purpose) flour
150ml/¼ pint/⅔ cup milk
150ml/¼ pint/⅔ cup water
2 eggs, beaten
vegetable oil, for deep-frying
caster (superfine) sugar or icing (confectioners') sugar, for dusting

churros taste **divine** dipped into **hot chocolate** – eat them any place, but especially when **sprawled** on the floor

Bring the milk to the boil in a small pan. When the chocolate has melted, remove it from the heat and stir in a little milk. Now whisk in the remaining milk – a hand-held blender is good for this – until frothy. Pour into mugs and drink hot. Remove the churros from the oven, roll in caster or icing sugar, pile into a basket and eat immediately, dipping them into the hot chocolate.

I've eaten versions of this in many coffee bars and, although delicious, have always thought "I could improve on that". Well, I have, and this is a dream to make with kids. They love smashing up the biscuits, and can do most of the rest, apart from melting the chocolate and lining the pan. I have to admit though, I too enjoy the contrast of melting chocolate chips, crunchy biscuits and soft marshmallows all blended together – it's not just kid's stuff.

rocky road **chocolate bars**

Line a 20cm/8in square cake pan, measuring about 2.5cm/1in deep, with baking parchment. Put the butter in a pan with the chocolate, sugar, syrup and cocoa powder. Place over a gentle heat until completely melted. Put the biscuits into a large plastic bag and smash with a rolling pin until broken up into rough chunks. Stir these into the chocolate mixture followed by the marshmallows and chocolate chips. Mix well together.

Spoon the mixture into the pan, but don't press down too much – it should look like a rocky road. Chill for at least 1 hour, or until firm. Remove from the pan and cut into 16 bars. If you like, dust the bars with icing sugar before serving.

makes 16 bars

225g/8oz/1 cup salted butter
115g/4oz dark (bittersweet) chocolate with more than 60% cocoa solids, roughly broken up
30ml/2 tbsp caster (superfine) sugar
30ml/2 tbsp golden (light corn) syrup
30ml/2 tbsp good quality (unsweetened) cocoa powder
350g/12oz mixed digestive biscuits (Graham crackers) and ginger nut biscuits
50g/2oz mini marshmallows
75g/3oz mixed white and milk chocolate chips
icing (confectioners') sugar, for dusting (optional)

Just the words egg nog suggest something rich and creamy. This drink has Scandinavian/ American origins and is usually served cold, but I've warmed it up to really bring out the flavour of the brandy and rum. Though a familiar name, I don't think that many know how to make an egg nog, so here it is in all its glory – with cinnamon sticks for stirring.

warm and creamy **egg nog**

serves 4

475ml/16fl oz/2 cups double
(heavy) cream
3 long strips orange rind
2.5ml/½ tsp freshly grated nutmeg
1 cinnamon stick
4 eggs, separated
30ml/2 tbsp caster
(superfine) sugar
175ml/6fl oz/¾ cup golden rum
250ml/8fl oz/1 cup brandy
extra grated nutmeg and
4 cinnamon sticks, to serve

Pour the cream into a small pan, add the orange rind, nutmeg and the cinnamon stick and bring slowly to the boil. In a mixing bowl, beat the egg yolks with the sugar until really pale and creamy. When the cream is boiling, pour on to the egg mixture and whisk well. Pour the mixture back into the pan and cook over a very gentle heat, stirring all the time, until it forms a custard as thick as pouring cream. Do not overheat or it will curdle.

Pour the rum and brandy into a pan and warm through. Stir into the egg custard. Whisk the egg whites until they form soft peaks and carefully fold into the warm custard. Pour into a warmed punch bowl (or just a pretty heatproof glass bowl). Sprinkle the surface of the egg nog with extra nutmeg to serve at the table or just ladle straight into warmed glasses or mugs. Put a cinnamon stick (to use as a stirrer) into each mug or glass before filling with egg nog.

Shortbread should always be in the biscuit tin or cookie jar – it is so moreish. As a Scot, I am very particular about my shortbread. It should melt in the mouth, taste buttery but never greasy, and always make you crave for more.

sugar-crusted **shortbread rounds**

makes about 24

450g/1lb/2 cups salted butter
225g/8oz/1 heaped cup caster
(superfine) sugar
450g/1lb/4 cups plain
(all-purpose) flour
225g/8oz/scant 1½ cups ground
rice or rice flour
5ml/1 tsp salt
demerara (raw) sugar, to decorate
golden caster (superfine) sugar,
for dusting

Preheat the oven to 190°C/375°F/Gas 5. Make sure all the ingredients are at room temperature. I like to use salted butter as it has more flavour than unsalted (sweet), but if you only have unsalted, then use it – don't make a special trip to the shops to buy some. In a food processor or bowl, cream the butter and sugar together until light, pale and fluffy. If you used a food processor, scrape the mixture out into a mixing bowl.

Sift together the flour, ground rice or rice flour and salt and stir into the butter and sugar with a wooden spoon, until the mixture resembles fine breadcrumbs. (The rice flour adds a toothsome grittiness and shortness to the dough, which distinguishes home-made shortbread from the bought variety.) Working quickly, gather the dough together with your hand, then put it on a clean work surface. Knead lightly together until it forms a ball but take care not to over-knead or the shortbread will be tough and greasy. Lightly roll into a sausage shape, about 7.5cm/3in thick. Wrap in cling film (plastic wrap) and chill until firm.

Pour the demerara sugar on to a sheet of baking parchment. Unwrap the dough and roll in the sugar until evenly coated. Using a large, sharp knife, slice the roll into discs about 1cm/½in thick.

Place the discs on to two baking sheets lined with baking parchment, spacing well apart. Bake for 20–25 minutes until very pale gold. (Shortbread should never really darken, but just set and turn a very pale colour.)

Remove from the oven and sprinkle with golden caster sugar. Allow to cool on the baking sheet for 10 minutes before transferring to a wire rack to cool completely.

there is something very satisfying about working with dough – it's the feel of the thing when rolling and shaping it

These luxurious little tarts are a well-established treat for my mother and myself after a hard day's shopping. Slippers on to tired feet, cups of tea and a nutmeg-dusted custard tart each, and we are ready to rustle through our purchases – girls in heaven.

little nutmeg **custard tarts**

Make the pastry first. Sift the flour and salt on to a sheet of baking parchment. Put the butter, sugar, egg yolks and vanilla essence in a food processor and process until the mixture resembles scrambled eggs. Tip in the flour and blend until just combined. Transfer the dough to a lightly floured surface and knead gently until smooth. Form into a ball, flatten and wrap in cling film (plastic wrap). Chill for at least 30 minutes. Bring back to room temperature before rolling out.

Roll out the pastry thinly and use to line eight individual 10cm/4in loose-based tart pans. (It is also nice to use smaller but deeper pans and make fewer tarts; just remember they will need slightly longer cooking.) Place the pans on a baking sheet and chill for 30 minutes.

Preheat the oven to 200°C/400°F/Gas 6. To make the custard filling, heat the milk in a pan until just warmed but not boiling. Beat the egg yolks and sugar together in a bowl until pale and creamy. Pour the milk on to the yolks and stir well to mix. Do not whisk as this will produce too many bubbles. Strain the milk mixture into a jug (pitcher) and pour into the tart cases.

Liberally grate fresh nutmeg over the surface of the tartlets. Bake for about 10 minutes, then lower the heat to 180°C/350°F/Gas 4 and bake for another 10 minutes, or until the filling has set and is just turning golden. Don't overbake as the tartlets should be a bit wobbly when they come out of the oven. Remove from the pans to cool slightly but serve warm.

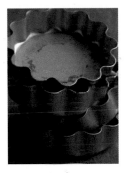

makes about 8

600ml/1 pint/2½ cups full cream (whole) milk
6 egg yolks
75g/3oz/6 tbsp caster (superfine) sugar
a whole nutmeg

For the rich butter pastry
175g/6oz/1½ cups plain (all-purpose) flour
a good pinch of salt
75g/3oz/6 tbsp unsalted (sweet) butter, at room temperature
75g/3oz/6 tbsp caster (superfine) sugar
3 egg yolks, at room temperature
2.5ml/½ tsp vanilla essence (extract)

at the table

Is there anything more cheering than sharing good food, drink and conversation with the people whose company you enjoy the most? Eating together, during the week at least, seems to be a disappearing routine, and meals more often resemble relay feeding than a relaxing time spent with others. If weekends are the only time to get together, make them an opportunity to prepare meals that will encourage friends and family to linger around the table.

To ensure this, food and drink should be as warm and welcoming as possible. It should suit all tastes, and there should be plenty of it. There's room for nostalgia here,

classic bread and butter pudding becomes
pain au chocolat and hazelnut pudding, and as for
traditional apple pie – well, it's been caramelized

with dishes such as old-fashioned steak and mushroom pudding and apple pie, but also the chance to try dishes from around the world, for example a spicy Thai curry. No dishing up in the kitchen, either – serve everything in big bowls and on generous platters. Soup brought to the table in a huge tureen, or even in the pot, looks

friendly and unpretentious, and ladling the soup into a warm bowl and passing it on is satisfying in itself. Two classics are featured here; cream of tomato soup and real chicken soup, which are so good when made at home.

If you are going to be cooking for a large number of people, you can go to town on heartier dishes that really only work when there's at least four of you sitting down to eat. Roast dinners seem to unite everyone, so I've included my recipe for perfect roast chicken with creamy baked potatoes and roasted garlic. Many of the dishes selected for this part of the book are my tried and trusted variations on familiar classics. Their origins and the techniques used to

make them are hidden deep in the past, but it's wonderful to think you are sharing in a culinary tradition when making these dishes, even if you make a few changes for personal preference or practicality. There's also something seductive about finding the familiar in a new guise, so classic fish pie becomes fabulous fish pie flavoured with dill and saffron, and a

perfectly
smooth, fluffy
potatoes made
golden
yellow
with saffron

steamed pudding goes Stateside with its maple syrup and pecan flavouring. Cassoulet, classic peasant fare, is given a lighter, more modern touch while retaining the original flavour and texture of the dish.

Some of the dishes take a while to put together, but this is due largely to the actual cooking time, not the preparation. So, while the food is cooking, you can concentrate on other tasks, secure in the knowledge that a delicious meal will be awaiting you at the end of the day. Time is precious, but to invest it in the making of a special meal is time spent well indeed.

Tomato soup is everybody's favourite… and my favourite came out of a can, until I made fresh tomato soup with sun-ripened tomatoes. What a revelation – fresh, but wonderfully warming and with an earthy richness hidden in its depths.

cream of tomato soup
with black olive ciabatta toasts

serves 6

450g/1lb very ripe tomatoes (preferably fresh rather than canned plum tomatoes)
30ml/2 tbsp olive oil
1 onion, chopped
1 garlic clove, crushed
30ml/2 tbsp sherry vinegar
30ml/2 tbsp tomato purée (paste)
15ml/1 tbsp cornflour (cornstarch) or potato flour
300ml/½ pint/1¼ cups passata (bottled strained tomatoes)
1 bay leaf
900ml/1½ pints/3¾ cups vegetable or chicken stock
200ml/7fl oz/scant 1 cup crème fraîche
salt and ground black pepper
basil leaves, to garnish

For the black olive ciabatta toasts
1 plain or black olive ciabatta
1 small red (bell) pepper
3 whole garlic cloves, skins on
225g/8oz black olives (preferably a wrinkly Greek variety)
30–45ml/2–3 tbsp salted capers or capers in vinegar
12 drained canned anchovy fillets or 1 small can tuna in oil, drained
about 150ml/¼ pint/⅔ cup good quality olive oil
fresh lemon juice and ground black pepper, to taste
45ml/3 tbsp chopped fresh basil

Make the ciabatta toasts first. Preheat the oven to 200°C/400°F/Gas 6. Split the ciabatta in half and cut each half into nine fingers to give 18 in total. Arrange on a baking sheet and bake for 10–15 minutes until golden and crisp. Place the whole pepper and garlic cloves under a hot grill (broiler) and grill (broil) for 15 minutes, turning, until charred all over. If you prefer, you can bake them in the oven for about 25 minutes. Once charred, put the garlic and pepper in a plastic bag, seal and leave to to cool for about 10 minutes.

When the pepper is cool, lightly rub off the skin (do not wash) and remove the stalk and seeds. Peel the skin off the garlic. Stone the olives (I use a cherry-stoner for this). Rinse the capers under running water, to remove the salt or vinegar. Place the prepared ingredients in a food processor with the anchovies or tuna and process until roughly chopped. With the machine running, slowly add the olive oil until you have a fairly smooth dark paste. Alternatively, just stir in the olive oil for a chunkier result. Season to taste with lemon juice and pepper. Stir in the basil. Spread the paste on the finger toasts, or, if not using immediately, transfer to a jar, cover with a layer of olive oil and keep in the refrigerator for up to three weeks.

Make the soup. If using fresh tomatoes, cut them in half and remove the seeds and pulp using a lemon squeezer. Press the tomato pulp through a sieve and reserve. Retain the tomato halves. Heat the oil in a pan and add the onion, garlic, sherry vinegar, tomato purée and the tomato halves or canned tomatoes, if using. Stir, then cover the pan and cook over a low heat for 1 hour until very soft. Stir from time to time. When done, pour the soup into a blender or food processor and process until smooth, then pass through a sieve to remove any pieces of skin. Return to the pan.

Mix the cornflour or potato flour with the reserved tomato pulp or 30ml/2 tbsp water until very smooth, then stir into the hot tomato soup with the passata, bay leaf and stock. Simmer for 30 minutes. Taste and adjust the seasoning. Stir in the crème fraîche and garnish with the basil leaves. Serve piping hot, with the ciabatta toasts.

ciabatta toast with salty black olives, a little roasted garlic and the silken texture of sweet red peppers complete the seduction

A real chicken soup, clear, golden and warming, filled with lightly cooked pasta, is not called Jewish penicillin for nothing – it really warms you up and it feels as if it is actually doing you good. This is one to bring steaming to the table in a big white soup tureen. It takes a little time to make, but this recipe never fails.

real old-fashioned chicken soup

Put the chicken, or guinea fowl and chicken pieces, into a large pan with all the vegetables and the bay leaf. Cover with 2.4 litres/4 pints/10 cups cold water. Bring slowly to the boil, carefully skimming off any scum that rises to the top. Add 5ml/1 tsp salt and some ground black pepper.

Turn down the heat and simmer the soup slowly for at least 2 hours, or until the fowl is tender. When simmering, the surface of the liquid should just tremble. If it boils, the soup will be cloudy.

When tender, remove the bird from the broth and strip the flesh off the carcass. (Use the meat in sandwiches or a risotto.) Return the bones to the soup and simmer gently for another hour.

Strain the soup into a bowl, cool, then chill overnight. The next day the soup should have set to a solid jelly and will be covered with a thin layer of solidified chicken fat. Carefully remove the fat. To serve the soup, reheat in a large pan. Add the vermicelli and chopped parsley, and simmer for 6–8 minutes until the pasta is cooked. Taste and season well. Serve piping hot.

serves 4–6

2kg/4½lb boiling fowl (stewing chicken) with giblets (except liver), or same weight of guinea fowl and chicken wings and thighs, mixed
I large onion, halved
2 large carrots, halved lengthways
6 celery sticks, roughly chopped
I bay leaf
175g/6oz vermicelli pasta
45ml/3 tbsp chopped fresh parsley or whole parsley leaves
salt and ground black pepper

this dish is forever linked with childhood – eating it while ill in bed, listening to the chatter drifting in from the dining room

This wonderfully comforting soup originates from Cullen, a fishing village in Scotland, and is traditionally made with Finnan haddock that has been cold-smoked until it is just the palest gold in colour. The fish is then combined with soft leeks and puréed potato to produce such a creamy concoction that one bowlful is rarely enough.

cullen skink

Put the haddock, skin-side up, in a shallow pan and cover with the onion slices, milk and water. Bring to just below boiling, turn down the heat and poach gently for about 10 minutes until cooked.

Meanwhile, boil the potatoes in salted water for 10–15 minutes, or until tender, then drain and mash. When the fish is cooked, strain the cooking liquid into a pan and reserve. Flake the fish and set aside. Whisk the mashed potato into the reserved fish liquid, stir in the leeks, bring to the boil and simmer for 10 minutes until the leeks are tender.

Whisk the cream and egg yolk together and stir into the soup. Reheat gently, without boiling, until slightly thickened. Gently stir in the reserved flaked fish, taste and adjust the seasoning, if necessary, and heat through. Stir the chopped parsley into the soup and serve piping hot, dotted with knobs (pats) of butter that will melt and run over the surface of the soup.

serves 4

900g/2lb undyed smoked haddock, preferably Finnan
1 onion, finely sliced
450ml/¾ pint/scant 2 cups milk
450ml/¾ pint/scant 2 cups water
450g/1lb floury potatoes, peeled and cut into large chunks
225g/8oz leeks, finely sliced
300ml/½ pint/1¼ cups single (light) cream
1 large (US extra large) egg yolk
30ml/2 tbsp chopped fresh parsley
50g/2oz/¼ cup butter
salt and ground black pepper

this is fish soup with
a delicate touch
– the pools of melted butter
are an essential indulgence

A recipe for roast chicken seems as familiar as toast, but can be equally difficult to get just right. Rubbing the outside of the bird with lemon, smearing it generously with butter and sprinkling with salt will give a beautiful deep brown, crisp skin, as well as keeping the flesh moist and succulent. The garlic roasts to a nutty melting softness.

perfect roast chicken with creamy baked potatoes and roasted garlic

serves 4

1.6kg/3½lb free-range
(farm-fresh) chicken
I lemon
2 bay leaves
a small bunch of fresh thyme
50g/2oz/¼ cup butter
salt and ground black pepper

For the creamy baked potatoes
50g/2oz/¼ cup butter
900g/2lb waxy potatoes, such as
Désirée or russet, peeled and
thinly sliced
115g/4oz/1⅓ cups freshly grated
Parmesan cheese
freshly grated nutmeg
I egg, beaten
300ml/½ pint/1¼ cups double
(heavy) cream
salt and ground black pepper

For the roasted garlic
4–6 garlic heads

Preheat the oven to 160°C/325°F/Gas 3. To make the baked potatoes, butter a shallow, flameproof dish. Layer the potatoes in the dish, sprinkling each layer with some of the cheese, nutmeg, and salt and pepper. I like to use Désirée potatoes as they have a lovely creamy texture, and will stick together nicely during cooking. More floury potatoes only disintegrate into mush. Beat the egg and cream together, and pour it over the potatoes. Sprinkle any remaining cheese over the top.

Put the dish on top of the stove and lightly warm it through before baking in the oven for about 1 hour, or until the potatoes are tender and the top is golden and crisp. (This dish reheats very well, so it is worth making before you roast the chicken to make sure it is perfectly cooked.) Remove from the oven.

Turn the oven up to 200°C/400°F/Gas 6. Untie any trussing and tuck the wings under the chicken. Remove any fat from the cavity. Cut the lemon in half and rub the cut halves all over the chicken. Tuck the lemons inside the cavity with the herbs. Spread the butter all over the breast and legs, seasoning well. Put the bird in a roasting pan.

Now prepare the garlic. Peel away some of the papery skin from each head. Lightly ease each head apart, but make sure the cloves are still attached. Sit the heads on a double sheet of kitchen foil and bring the foil up to form a parcel. Pour in 45ml/3 tbsp water and close the parcel. Seal and place in the oven to roast with the chicken.

After 45 minutes, remove the roasting pan from the oven, lift out and open the bag of garlic and set it on a baking dish. Return the chicken to the oven and cook for another 15 minutes, or until starting to go brown. Test the chicken to see if it is cooked, by inserting a skewer into the thickest part of the thigh. If the juices run clear, it is cooked, but if they are still pink, cook for another 10–15 minutes. Allow the bird to rest in the turned off oven for 15 minutes before carving.

Remove the chicken from the oven and pour out any juices caught in the cavity into the pan. Serve the chicken with the cooking juices, the roasted garlic and the creamy baked potatoes.

This is my idea of the ultimate fish pie. Breaking through the golden potato crust reveals perfectly cooked plump prawns and hearty chunks of cod swathed in a creamy parsley sauce. Cook in a big dish and bring triumphantly to the table.

fabulous fish pie
with saffron and dill mash

Put the milk, onion, bay leaf and peppercorns into a large pan. Bring to the boil, then simmer for about 10 minutes. Set aside.

Lay the cod and haddock fillets, skin-side up, in a roasting pan. Strain over the milk and simmer for 5–7 minutes on the stovetop until just opaque. Lift the fish out of the milk and transfer to a plate. Reserve the milk.

When the fish is cool enough to handle, pull off the skin and flake the flesh into large pieces, removing any bones as you go. Transfer to a large bowl and add the shelled prawns.

Melt the butter in a small pan. Stir in the flour and cook for a minute or so, then gradually stir in the flavoured milk from the roasting pan until you achieve a smooth consistency. Whisk well and simmer gently for 15 minutes until thick and a little reduced, then taste and season with salt and pepper. Stir in the parsley.

Pour the sauce over the fish. Carefully mix together, transfer the mixture to a pie dish and leave to cool.

Preheat the oven to 180°C/350°F/Gas 4. To make the saffron and dill mash, boil the potatoes in salted water until tender, drain well and mash. Lump-free mashed potatoes are an essential here – I press them through a sieve to make sure they're really smooth. Using an electric whisk, beat in the saffron and its soaking water, then the butter, milk and dill to make mashed potato that is light and fluffy. When the fish mixture has set, spoon over the golden mash, piling it on top. Bake for 30–40 minutes, or until the potato is golden brown and crisp. Serve immediately.

serves 6

750ml/1¼ pints/3 cups milk
1 onion, chopped
1 bay leaf
2–3 peppercorns
450g/1lb each of fresh cod fillet
and smoked haddock fillet, skin on
350g/12oz cooked tiger prawns
(shrimp), shelled, with tails left on
75g/3oz/6 tbsp butter
75g/3oz/¾ cup plain
(all-purpose) flour
60ml/4 tbsp chopped fresh parsley
salt and ground black pepper

For the saffron and dill mash
1.3kg/3lb floury potatoes, peeled
large pinch saffron threads, soaked
in 45ml/3 tbsp hot water
75g/3oz/6 tbsp butter
250ml/8fl oz/1 cup milk
45ml/3 tbsp chopped fresh dill

Cassoulet is peasant food originating from the south-west of France. It's a very hearty, one-pot meal of white beans, preserved meats and sausage. There is no definitive recipe, though the method of adding each meat at different stages to the simmering pot of beans and flavourings is crucial to the finished dish. I have lightened the stew and shortened the cooking time – traditionally, it is meant to go on bubbling for days – and it is usually served straight from the cooking pot.

butter bean **cassoulet**

serves 6–8

675g/1½lb/3¾ cups dried butter (lima) beans
2 large onions, sliced
6 large garlic cloves, crushed
3 bay leaves
10ml/2 tsp dried thyme
2 whole cloves
60ml/4 tbsp tomato purée (paste)
12 sun-dried tomatoes in oil, drained and roughly chopped
450g/1lb smoked pancetta in a piece
60ml/4 tbsp olive oil
4 boneless duck breasts
12 Toulouse or chunky Italian sausages
400g/14oz can plum tomatoes
75g/3oz/1½ cups stale white breadcrumbs
salt and ground black pepper

Put the beans in a large bowl, cover with plenty of cold water and leave to soak for several hours or overnight.

Drain the beans well and tip into a large pan. Cover with fresh water and bring to the boil. Boil rapidly for 10 minutes to destroy any indigestible enzymes, then drain well and tip into a large flameproof casserole. Add the onions, garlic, bay leaves, dried thyme, cloves, tomato purée and sun-dried tomatoes.

Trim the rind from the pancetta and cut into large pieces. Heat about 30ml/2 tbsp of the oil in a frying pan and brown the pancetta in batches. Stir it into the casserole and add enough water to cover. Bring to the boil, then reduce the heat so that it just simmers. Cover and simmer for about 1½ hours until the beans are tender.

Preheat the oven to 180°C/350°F/Gas 4. Score the skin of the duck breasts, then cut each breast into large pieces. Cut each sausage into three pieces. Heat the remaining oil in a frying pan and fry the duck, skin-side down, until golden brown, then transfer to the casserole. Lightly fry the sausages in the remaining fat and stir into the beans with the canned tomatoes, adding salt and pepper to taste.

Sprinkle the breadcrumbs in an even layer over the surface of the cassoulet and bake for 45–60 minutes, or until a golden crust has formed. Serve warm.

well made and not rushed, this is hard to beat – good rib-sticking stuff for large numbers

Although a true British classic, the suet crust pudding isn't made much nowadays, but it is another of those glorious things to cook for a special occasion. I fill it with lean beef, dried porcini and fresh mushrooms, and scent the suet crust heavily with lemon and herbs, especially thyme. While it steams away, the aroma is amazing.

steak and mushroom pudding
with a herby suet crust

Preheat the oven to 180°C/350°F/Gas 4. Drain the porcini mushrooms, reserving the soaking liquid, and roughly chop. Cut the steak into large cubes, then toss the steak with the flour and plenty of salt and pepper.

Heat the oil in a large, heavy frying pan until very hot. Add the onion and cook, stirring frequently until golden brown. Using a slotted spoon, transfer the onions to an ovenproof casserole. Fry the floured steak in batches until well browned on all sides.

Add the meat to the casserole with the chopped porcini and the fresh mushrooms and stir well. Pour in the reserved soaking liquid, wine and stock, add the mushroom ketchup, if using, and tuck in the bay leaf. Cover and cook in the oven for 1½ hours, until the meat is tender. Allow the mixture to cool completely.

To make the herby suet crust, butter a deep 1.7 litre/3 pint/7 cup ovenproof bowl. Sift the flour, baking powder and 2.5ml/½ tsp salt into a large mixing bowl. Stir in the herbs and lemon rind and season with plenty of pepper. Stir in the suet and butter. Make a well in the centre, add the egg, lemon juice and enough of the cold water to mix and gather into a soft but manageable dough.

Knead the dough lightly on a well-floured work surface. Cut off a quarter of the dough and wrap in cling film (plastic wrap). Shape the rest into a ball and roll out into a large round, big enough to line the ovenproof bowl. Lift up the dough and drop it into the bowl, pressing against the sides to line the bowl evenly. Roll out the reserved pastry to a round large enough to use as a lid.

Spoon in the beef filling to within 1cm/½in of the rim. Top up with the gravy. (Keep the remaining gravy to serve with the pudding later.) Dampen the edges of the pastry and fit the lid. Press the edges to seal and trim away the excess pastry. Cover with pleated, buttered baking parchment, then with pleated foil to allow for the crust to rise. Tie string under the lip of the basin to hold the paper in place, then take it over the top to form a handle. Place the bowl in a large pan of simmering water, cover and steam for 1½ hours, topping up with boiling water as necessary. Bring the bowl to the table wrapped in a clean dishtowel and serve the pudding straight from the bowl.

serves 6

25g/1oz/½ cup dried porcini mushrooms, soaked in warm water for 20 minutes
1.3kg/3lb rump (round) steak, trimmed
30ml/2 tbsp plain (all-purpose) flour
30ml/2 tbsp olive or sunflower oil
1 large onion, chopped
225g/8oz chestnut or open cup mushrooms, halved or quartered if large
300ml/½ pint/1¼ cups fruity red wine
300ml/½ pint/1¼ cups beef stock
45ml/3 tbsp mushroom ketchup
1 bay leaf

For the herby suet crust
275g/10oz/2½ cups self-raising (self-rising) flour
5ml/1 tsp baking powder
15ml/1 tbsp each finely chopped fresh parsley, sage, rosemary and thyme
finely grated rind of 1 lemon
75g/3oz/1½ cups beef or vegetable suet
50g/2oz/¼ cup butter, chilled and grated
1 egg, beaten
juice of ½ lemon
150ml/¼ pint/⅔ cup cold water
salt and ground black pepper

A tagine is really only a stew simmered for a long time in the dish of the same name, and is perfect when you are catering for a crowd – you just leave it to cook.

lamb shanks and apricots
with minted sesame couscous

Melt the butter in a large, flameproof casserole. Brown the lamb shanks all over, three at a time, then transfer to a plate. Stir the onion and spices into the pan juices and cook for 5 minutes to release their aroma, and soften the onion. Add 2.5ml/½ tsp salt and plenty of pepper. Stir in the ground almonds.

Return the lamb to the pan with the orange rind and cover with 1.2 litres/2 pints/5 cups water. Bring to the boil, then turn the heat to very low. Cover the surface of the stew with a sheet of crumpled baking parchment, then the lid (this will prevent too much liquid escaping during the cooking). Simmer for 1 hour.

After this time, add the apricots, prunes and raisins, stir them into the liquid, recover and simmer for another hour. Just before serving, prepare the minted sesame couscous. Put the couscous into a measuring jug (cup) and note the measurement. Transfer to a bowl and measure out twice its volume in boiling water.

serves 6

50g/2oz/¼ cup butter
6 lamb shanks
1 onion, finely chopped
2.5ml/½ tsp ground cumin
2.5ml/½ tsp ground ginger
2.5ml/½ tsp ground cinnamon
10ml/2 tsp paprika
4 cloves
115g/4oz/1 cup ground almonds
3 large strips orange rind
225g/8oz/1 cup dried apricots
115g/4oz/½ cup stoned (pitted)
dried prunes
115g/4oz/scant 1 cup muscatel raisins
30ml/2 tbsp orange flower
water (optional)

the **spicy mixture** simmers for hours, concentrating the flavours and **thickening the sauce**

Stir the butter and mint into the boiling water, then pour evenly over the couscous. Cover tightly with cling film (plastic wrap) and leave to stand for 5 minutes.

Meanwhile, toast the sesame seeds in a frying pan until golden brown. Set aside. Uncover the couscous and, using a fork, fluff up the grains. Fork in the sesame seeds, taste and season well. When the lamb is ready it should be falling off the bone, the fruits should be plump and the sauce thickened. Taste the lamb for seasoning and add orange flower water, if using. Serve with the couscous.

For the minted sesame couscous
375g/13oz quick-cook couscous
115g/4oz/½ cup butter, cubed
60ml/4 tbsp chopped fresh mint
45ml/3 tbsp sesame seeds

The secret of a great Thai curry is not to be mean with the herbs and flavourings, and to get a balance between ginger, chilli and garlic. The aroma when making the paste is fabulous and even better when you start to cook.

thai green chicken curry
with coconut basil rice

serves 6

6 boneless, skinless chicken breasts
1 litre/1¾ pints/4 cups chicken stock
400ml/14fl oz can coconut milk
45ml/3 tbsp chopped fresh coriander (cilantro)
salt
shredded spring onions (scallions) and shredded red (bell) pepper, to serve

For the Thai green curry paste
5 fresh green chillies, seeded and chopped
6 shallots, chopped
3 garlic cloves
75g/3oz fresh coriander (cilantro)
finely grated rind of 1 lime
5ml/1 tsp dried shrimp paste
small piece of fresh root ginger, finely chopped
1 small stick lemon grass, chopped
2.5ml/½ tsp ground turmeric
2.5ml/½ tsp ground cumin
10ml/2 tsp ground coriander
30ml/2 tbsp vegetable oil
ground black pepper

For the coconut basil rice
350g/12oz/1½ cups basmati or Thai fragrant rice
12 large basil leaves (preferably Thai basil)
45ml/3 tbsp sunflower oil
45ml/3 tbsp black mustard seeds
5ml/1 tsp salt
400ml/14fl oz can coconut milk

Make the green curry paste. Put all the ingredients in a food processor or blender and process until smooth. (If making in advance, pack it into an airtight jar and store in the refrigerator for up to one month.)

To make the coconut rice, put the rice in a sieve and wash under cold running water until the water runs clear. Drain well. Tear the basil into pieces. Heat the oil in a non-stick pan, add the mustard seeds and cook for 1–2 minutes until the seeds start to pop. Stir in the rice and salt until well coated with the oil, then add the coconut milk and 350ml/12fl oz/1½ cups water. Bring to the boil, stir well, then simmer, uncovered, for 10–15 minutes.

Stir the basil into the rice, cover tightly and leave for about 10 minutes. Fluff up the rice with a fork before serving.

Make the chicken curry while the rice is cooking. Slice the chicken into strips. Whisk 250ml/8fl oz/1 cup of the stock and all the curry paste together in a frying pan and bring to the boil. Simmer for 2 minutes, or until all the liquid has evaporated.

Add the chicken and the remaining stock and stir well. Bring to the boil, turn down the heat and simmer gently for 10 minutes. Pour in the coconut milk, stir well and simmer for 5 minutes. Add the chopped coriander, taste and season with salt.

Serve the curry scattered with shredded spring onions and red pepper, and accompany with the coconut basil rice.

wonderfully fresh-tasting and full of tantalizing flavours

I can never resist a really good apple pie. If you use eating apples bursting with flavour, loads of butter and sugar, and make your own shortcrust pastry, then you can't go wrong. However, adding a buttery caramel to the apples takes it one step further and, coupled with the mixed spice, gives a rich flavour to the juices in the pie.

deep dish **apple pie**

Preheat the oven to 200°C/400°F/Gas 6. Make the pastry first. Sift together the flour and salt into a bowl. Rub in the lard or fat and butter until the mixture resembles fine breadcrumbs. Stir in enough chilled water to bring the pastry together. Knead lightly then wrap in cling film (plastic wrap) and chill for 30 minutes.

To make the filling, peel, core and thickly slice the apples. Melt the butter in a frying pan, add the sugar and cook for 3–4 minutes allowing it to melt and caramelize. Add the apples and stir around to coat. Cook over a brisk heat until the apples take on a little colour, add the spices and tip out into a bowl to cool slightly.

Divide the pastry in two and, on a lightly floured surface, roll out into two rounds that will easily fit a deep 23cm/9in pie plate. Line the plate with one round of pastry. Spoon in the cooled filling and mound up in the centre. Cover the apples with the remaining pastry, sealing and crimping the edges. Make a 5cm/2in long slit through the top of the pastry to allow the steam to escape. Brush the pie with milk and dredge with caster sugar.

Place the pie on a baking sheet and bake in the oven for 25–35 minutes until golden and firm. Serve with clotted cream, ice cream or double cream.

serves 6

900g/2lb eating apples
75g/3oz/6 tbsp unsalted
(sweet) butter
45–60ml/3–4 tbsp demerara
(raw) sugar
3 cloves
2.5ml/½ tsp mixed
(apple pie) spice

For the pastry
250g/9oz/2¼ cups plain
(all-purpose) flour
pinch of salt
50g/2oz/¼ cup lard or white
cooking fat, chilled and diced
75g/3oz/6 tbsp unsalted (sweet)
butter, chilled and diced
30–45ml/2–3 tbsp chilled water
a little milk, for brushing
caster (superfine) sugar,
for dredging
clotted cream, ice cream or double
(heavy) cream, to serve

Imagine a hot sponge cake, straight out of the oven but with less golden crust, a deeper sponge and more crumbliness – that's a steamed pudding. It can be flavoured with anything – maple syrup and pecan nuts are wonderful, and look superb when turned out, as here. Serve with lots of your own home-made custard.

sticky maple and pecan **steamed pud**

Butter a 900ml/1½ pint/3¾ cup heatproof pudding bowl generously. Stir the maple syrup, breadcrumbs and pecans together and spoon into the bowl.

Cream the butter with the orange rind and sugar until light and fluffy. Gradually beat in the eggs, then fold in the flour and salt. Stir in enough milk to make a loose mixture that will drop off the spoon if lightly shaken.

Carefully spoon the mixture into the bowl on top of the syrup and nuts. Cover with pleated, buttered baking parchment, then with pleated foil (the pleats allow for expansion). Tie string under the lip of the basin to hold the paper in place, then take it over the top to form a handle. Place the bowl in a pan of simmering water, cover and steam for 2 hours, topping up with boiling water as necessary. Remove the string, foil and paper, then turn out the pudding and serve with extra maple syrup and custard.

serves 6

60ml/4 tbsp pure maple syrup
30ml/2 tbsp fresh brown breadcrumbs
115g/4oz/1 cup shelled pecan nuts,
roughly chopped
115g/4oz/½ cup butter, softened
finely grated rind of 1 orange
115g/4oz/heaped ½ cup golden caster
(superfine) sugar
2 eggs, beaten
175g/6oz/1½ cups self-raising
(self-rising) flour, sifted
pinch of salt
about 75ml/5 tbsp milk
extra maple syrup and home-made
custard, to serve

 When I explain the ingredients of this pudding to guests, there is usually a sharp intake of breath and a cry of "That's outrageous!" Well – it is, and all the better for it. This is the most decadent version of classic bread and butter pudding I know, and it is equally at home as an informal indulgence and as a real dinner party treat.

hazelnut pain au chocolat pudding

serves 6

4 large pain au chocolats
75g/3oz chocolate and
hazelnut spread

For the custard
300ml/½ pint/1¼ cups milk
300ml/½ pint/1¼ cups double
(heavy) cream
1 vanilla pod (bean), split
6 egg yolks
115g/4oz/heaped ½ cup caster
(superfine) sugar
icing (confectioners') sugar,
for dusting
pouring cream, to serve

Butter a 1.7 litre/3 pint/7½ cup shallow baking dish. Cut the pain au chocolats into thick slices, then spread them with the chocolate and hazelnut spread. Arrange the slices, spread-side up and overlapping, in the prepared dish.

To make the custard, pour the milk and cream into a pan. Add the vanilla pod and place over a very low heat for 5 minutes until the mixture is almost boiling and well flavoured with vanilla.

Meanwhile, in a large bowl, whisk together the egg yolks and caster sugar until light and creamy. Strain the flavoured milk on to the egg mixture, whisking well. Pour the egg mixture evenly over the pain au chocolat and allow to stand for 10 minutes to allow the pain au chocolat to absorb the liquid. Preheat the oven to 180°C/350°F/Gas 4.

Place the baking dish in a large roasting pan and pour in enough boiling water to come half-way up the sides of the dish. Bake the pudding for 45–50 minutes until the custard is softly set and the top is crisp and golden brown.

Remove from the oven and leave the pudding in the roasting pan of water until just warm. Sprinkle with the icing sugar and serve with cream.

the creamy custard mingles with soft and buttery pain au chocolats that simply ooze with melting chocolate praline

on the sofa

Sometimes you just don't feel like sitting at a table to eat. Either it's too late or you're too tired, and all you want to do is kick off your shoes and sit back with something tasty. The sofa is just the place for this, particularly if the food is full of flavour and easy to eat with your fingers, a fork or chopsticks.

Food should be served in deep bowls or on large plates to avoid spills. You don't want to have to concentrate on eating your food when on the sofa, but you do want soothing tastes and contrasting textures to lull you into a relaxed mood. A silky smooth chickpea soup, drizzled with spiced butter and served with crisp tortilla chips is just the thing. Another excellent choice is prawn laksa – a savoury coconut broth that is brimming with prawns, vegetables and noodles, designed to both nourish and stimulate. Served in big bowls, you can slurp and crunch away to your heart's content.

a bowl of creamy heaven, bursting with fresh flavours

Rich and filling stews with chunky ingredients that can be easily scooped up with a spoon or fork are also always good for sofa-feasts. I've created a chunky cod and white bean stew for the occasion, flavoured with bacon, tomatoes and *pimentón* (a smoked paprika that is quite exquisite). Equally suitable is risotto – a rich and creamy meal in a bowl that is the original fork food. This one is made from sweet butternut squash, fresh rosemary, Parmesan cheese and a little chilli, and is just bursting with great flavours. Or try pasta, smothered in a rich chorizo and tomato sauce.

Tortilla (Spanish omelette) is another old sofa favourite. Its the kind of meal that can be made in one big pan and brought to the coffee table to be dished

this really is eating in the **comfort zone** – one-pot
meals are **the answer** – no fuss and no extras –
so curl up, relax and pull near the coffee table

out and eaten with a fork, so is perfect for casual dining.
It can be prepared very quickly if you cook the potatoes
and roast the peppers ahead of time.

Pizza is one of the easiest things to eat on the sofa, but
forget sending out for one. Make your own and you can
guarantee the base will be perfectly crisp every time (roll
out the dough very thinly and bake on a preheated baking
tray), and you can put as much or as little topping on it as
you like. Then all you have to do is slice and serve – the
bigger the wedges the better.

My one concession to salads appears in this chapter: a
warm tuna niçoise made with seared tuna. It makes a delicious meal-in-a-bowl,
and the flavours and textures are so comforting, it deserved recognition.

If all you want is to lie back with something
sweet, opt for the rhubarb and raspberry almond
crumble. With all that fruit, it just has to be good
for you. Like the savoury dishes, simplicity is the
key to the desserts. They are cooked in one dish,
making it easy to pile servings generously into
bowls. Most of these recipes are for two, but some
are intended for those occasions when friends
gather, in need of some culinary comforting.

This silky smooth nutty soup is so easy to make. Take it to the sofa with a bowl of warm and spicy tortilla chips and dip, crunch and slurp your way through your favourite television fix.

bacon and chickpea soup
with tortilla chips

serves 4–6

400g/14oz/2 cups dried chickpeas, soaked overnight in cold water
115g/4oz/½ cup butter
150g/5oz pancetta or streaky (fatty) bacon, roughly chopped
2 onions, finely chopped
1 carrot, chopped
1 celery stick, chopped
15ml/1 tbsp chopped fresh rosemary
2 fresh bay leaves
2 garlic cloves, halved

For the tortilla chips
75g/3oz/6 tbsp butter
2.5ml/½ tsp sweet paprika
1.5ml/¼ tsp ground cumin
175g/6oz plain tortilla chips
salt and ground black pepper

Drain the chickpeas, put them in a large pan and cover with plenty of cold water. Bring to the boil and simmer for about 20 minutes. Strain and set aside.

Melt the butter in a large pan and add the pancetta or bacon. Fry over a medium heat until just beginning to turn golden. Add the chopped vegetables and cook for 5–10 minutes until soft.

Add the chickpeas to the pan with the chopped rosemary, bay leaves, halved garlic cloves and enough water to cover completely. Bring to the boil, half cover, turn down the heat and simmer for 45–60 minutes, stirring occasionally. (The chickpeas should start to disintegrate and will thicken the soup.)

Allow the soup to cool slightly, then pour it into a blender or food processor and process until smooth. Return the soup to the rinsed-out pan, taste and season with salt and plenty of black pepper. Reheat gently.

To make the tortilla chips, preheat the oven to 180°C/350°F/Gas 4. Melt the butter with the paprika and cumin in a pan, then lightly brush the mixture over the tortilla chips. Reserve any left over spiced butter. Spread the chips out on a baking sheet and warm through in the oven for 5 minutes.

Ladle the soup into bowls, pour some reserved spiced butter over each serving and sprinkle with a little paprika. Serve with the warm tortilla chips.

a silky smooth, nutty soup with hints of smoky bacon, finished with a swirl of melted spiced butter

It's sometimes nice to dine away from the table and this is just the no-nonsense dish to do it with. Everything is cooked in one pot – the chunks of fresh, flaky cod, made yellow with saffron, are added at the last minute, and their flavour is offset by the smoked paprika-spiced beans. A big pile of crusty bread wouldn't go amiss.

cod and bean stew
with saffron and paprika

Preheat the grill (broiler) and line the pan with foil. Halve the red pepper and scoop out the seeds. Place, cut-side down, in the grill pan and grill (broil) under a hot heat for about 10–15 minutes, until the skin is charred.

Put the pepper into a plastic bag, seal and leave for 10 minutes to steam. Remove from the bag, peel off the skin and discard. Chop the pepper into large pieces.

Heat the olive oil in a pan, then add the bacon and garlic. Fry for 2 minutes, then add the sliced onion. Cover the pan and cook for about 5 minutes until the onion is soft. Stir in the paprika and *pimentón*, the saffron and its soaking water, and salt and pepper.

Stir the beans into the pan and add just enough stock to cover. Bring to the boil and simmer, uncovered, for about 15 minutes, stirring occasionally to prevent sticking. Stir in the chopped pepper and tomato quarters. Drop in the cubes of cod and bury them in the sauce. Cover and simmer for 5 minutes until cooked. Stir in the chopped coriander. Serve the stew in warmed soup plates or bowls, garnished with the coriander sprigs. Eat with lots of crusty bread.

serves 6–8

1 large red (bell) pepper
45ml/3 tbsp olive oil
4 rashers (strips) streaky (fatty) bacon, roughly chopped
4 garlic cloves, finely chopped
1 onion, sliced
10ml/2 tsp paprika
5ml/1 tsp hot *pimentón* (smoked Spanish paprika)
large pinch of saffron threads or 1 sachet powdered saffron, soaked in 45ml/3 tbsp hot water
400g/14oz jar Spanish butter (lima) beans (*judias del barco* or *judias blancas guisadas*) or canned haricot (navy) beans, drained and rinsed
about 600ml/1 pint/2½ cups fish stock, or water and 60ml/4 tbsp Thai fish sauce
6 plum tomatoes, quartered
350g/12oz fresh skinned cod fillet, cut into large chunks
45ml/3 tbsp chopped fresh coriander (cilantro), plus a few sprigs to garnish
salt and ground black pepper
crusty bread, to serve

My friend Stefan, who is a champion laksa maker, always keeps home-made stock in the freezer specially for the purpose of making instant, late-night meals. This is a hearty dish, and is perfect when you are tired. Tiger prawns, vegetables and noodles are tangled together in a savoury coconut broth – flavours and textures that both soothe and stimulate the appetite.

aromatic **prawn laksa**

serves 4

6 dried red chillies
1 onion, chopped
1 small piece fresh root ginger, peeled and grated
5ml/1 tsp ground turmeric
45ml/3 tbsp Thai fish sauce
finely grated rind of 1 lime
8 macadamia nuts
5ml/1 tsp ground coriander
60ml/4 tbsp vegetable oil
475ml/16fl oz/2 cups fish stock
750ml/1¼ pints/3 cups coconut milk from a can or carton
225g/8oz dried flat rice noodles
60ml/4 tbsp thick coconut milk, made by dissolving grated creamed coconut in boiling water, or 120ml/4fl oz/½ cup coconut cream
400g/14oz raw headless tiger prawns (shrimp), shelled and deveined but with tails left intact
225g/8oz/4 cups fresh beansprouts
coriander (cilantro) sprigs, to serve

Soak the chillies in warm water for 30 minutes. Drain them, cut them in half and remove the seeds. Put the chillies, onion, ginger, turmeric, fish sauce, lime rind, macadamia nuts, ground coriander and half of the vegetable oil into a food processor or blender and process to form a smooth paste.

Heat the remaining oil in a pan, add the paste and fry for 5 minutes, stirring all the time to prevent sticking. Add the fish stock and simmer for a further 5 minutes.

Pour in the canned coconut milk, stirring constantly to prevent curdling. Bring to the boil and simmer, uncovered, for about 5 minutes. Meanwhile, cook the noodles in a separate pan of boiling water according to the packet instructions, drain and toss in a little oil. Set aside.

Stir the thick coconut milk and prawns into the soup. Simmer for a further 2–3 minutes.

To serve, put a pile of noodles into four deep serving bowls. Add the beansprouts and prawns, and pour over the hot soup. Top with the coriander and serve immediately.

I'm afraid you can't help slurping this – but **what are noodles for** if not for slurping?

Once you've tasted a really good home-made pizza there's no going back to ready-made ones. When you make your own you have total control over the results. This one I make regularly for myself – gooey smoked cheese and ham on a bed of onions, dripping off a thin and crispy base. The rocket is thrown on top to wilt into the cheese.

smoked mozzarella and ham pizza with rocket

To make the dough, cream the fresh yeast with the sugar in a medium bowl and whisk in 250ml/8fl oz/1cup warm water. Leave for 10 minutes until frothy. If using another type of yeast, follow the manufacturer's instructions.

Sift the flour into a large bowl and make a well in the centre. Pour in the yeast mixture, olive oil and salt. Mix together with a round-bladed knife, then use your hands to form a soft dough.

Tip the dough out on to a lightly floured surface and knead for 10 minutes until smooth and elastic. The dough should be quite soft, but if it is too soft to handle, add more flour. Place in a clean, oiled bowl, cover with a damp dishtowel and leave to rise for about 1 hour until doubled in bulk.

To make the pizza topping, heat the oil in a pan and add the onions. Cook over a gentle heat for about 20 minutes, stirring occasionally, until the onions are soft and golden. (They must not brown or they will lose their clean, soft, sweet taste.) Stir in the herbs and season with salt and pepper.

Preheat the oven to 240°C/475°F/Gas 9. Knock back (punch down) the pizza dough. Divide the dough in half and roll out to make two rounds 25–30cm/10–12in in diameter, and about 5mm/¼in thick. Slide these on to two well-floured, flat baking sheets.

Cover the pizza bases evenly with the onions. Scatter over the smoked ham and lay the mozzarella on top. Sprinkle with the Parmesan cheese. Bake in the oven for about 15 minutes until golden and crisp. Pile the rocket on top and serve immediately.

makes two pizzas

75ml/5 tbsp olive oil
1kg/2¼lb onions, finely sliced
15ml/1 tbsp chopped fresh
rosemary
10ml/2 tsp dried oregano
115g/4oz sliced smoked ham,
torn into pieces
1 smoked mozzarella, peeled and
thinly sliced
30ml/2 tbsp freshly grated
Parmesan cheese
100g/4oz rocket (arugula)
salt and ground black pepper

For the pizza dough
25g/1oz fresh yeast, 15g/½oz dried
active baking yeast or 2 sachets
easy-blend (rapid-rise) dried yeast
a pinch of sugar
350g/12oz/3 cups Italian "00" flour,
plus extra, for dusting
30ml/2 tbsp olive oil, plus extra for
brushing and drizzling
5ml/1 tsp salt

there are few things more pleasurable than kneading a yeasty dough until shiny and elastic – it's really quite a sensual thing

A pasta sauce should be rich, thick and robust. I love the assertive flavours of chorizo sausage, and the combination with tomatoes, red wine and olive oil, simmered for ages, is just delicious.

rich tomato and chorizo sauce with pasta

Peel off the casing from the chorizo and cut it into chunks. Put in a blender or food processor and process until just broken down. Squeeze the sausage meat out of the skins into a bowl and break up the meat. Stir in the chorizo.

Heat the oil in a pan, then add the onion and garlic, and cook for 5 minutes until soft and golden. Stir in the sausage meat, browning it all over and breaking up any lumps with a wooden spoon. Pour in the passata and wine, and add the remaining ingredients except the pasta and Parmesan. Stir well and bring to the boil. Turn down the heat, half cover the pan and simmer very gently for at least 1 hour, stirring occasionally, until the oil separates out to form a film on the top and the sauce is reduced. When the sauce is almost ready, cook the pasta in a pan of salted boiling water until just tender, then drain. Season the sauce well and toss with the cooked pasta. Serve with the Parmesan cheese.

serves 4

225g/8oz fresh chorizo sausage
225g/8oz fresh Italian sausages or good butchers' sausages
30ml/2 tbsp olive oil
1 onion, finely chopped
2 garlic cloves, finely chopped
450ml/¾ pint/scant 2 cups passata (bottled strained tomatoes)
150ml/¼ pint/⅔ cup dry red wine
30ml/2 tbsp tomato purée (paste)
6 sun-dried tomatoes, chopped
15ml/1 tbsp chopped fresh rosemary
30ml/2 tbsp chopped fresh sage
salt and ground black pepper
450g/1lb/4 cups dried pasta
freshly grated Parmesan cheese, for sprinkling

This is one of those dishes that you forget just how good it is – until you make it again. It relies on only a few basic ingredients, but the mixture of eggs, potatoes and silky peppers is always soothing.

roasted red pepper tortilla

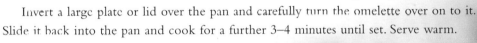

Season the potatoes well with salt and pepper. Heat half the oil in a non-stick frying pan and cook the potatoes over a medium heat for 15 minutes until starting to brown.

Meanwhile, in another pan, heat half the remaining oil and fry the onion slices for about 20 minutes until really soft. Grill (broil) the peppers for 10 minutes until charred on the outside. Put into a plastic bag, seal and leave for 10 minutes to steam.

Beat the eggs in a bowl, add the potatoes and onions and stir well. Season to taste. Peel the skins off the peppers, roughly chop the flesh and add to the potato mixture.

Heat the remaining oil in the non-stick frying pan and pour in the egg and potato mixture. Cook over a low heat for about 10–15 minutes until beginning to set.

Invert a large plate or lid over the pan and carefully turn the omelette over on to it. Slide it back into the pan and cook for a further 3–4 minutes until set. Serve warm.

serves 2

450g/1lb potatoes, peeled and cut
into small chunks
50ml/2fl oz/¼ cup olive oil
1 large onion, thinly sliced
2 red (bell) peppers, halved
and seeded
4 eggs
salt and ground black pepper

A dangerously rich and creamy risotto. The pumpkin gradually disintegrates to speckle the rice with orange. The rosemary gives it a sweet pungency, while garlic and chilli add bite.

pumpkin, rosemary and chilli **risotto**

serves 4

115g/4oz/½ cup butter
1 small onion, finely chopped
2 large garlic cloves, crushed
1 fresh red chilli, seeded and finely chopped
250g/9oz fresh pumpkin or butternut squash, peeled and roughly chopped
30ml/2 tbsp chopped fresh rosemary
250g/9oz/1½ cups risotto rice, preferably Arborio or Vialone Nano
about 750ml/1¼ pints/3 cups hot chicken stock, preferably fresh
50g/2oz/⅔ cup freshly grated Parmesan cheese, plus extra to serve
salt and ground black pepper

Melt half the butter in a heavy pan, add the onion and garlic, and cook for 10 minutes until softening. Add the chilli and cook for about 1 minute. Add the pumpkin or squash and cook, stirring constantly, for 5 minutes. Stir in the rosemary.

Add the rice, and stir with a wooden spoon to coat with the oil and vegetables. Cook for 2–3 minutes to toast the rice grains.

Begin to add the stock, a large ladleful at a time, stirring all the time until each ladleful has been absorbed into the rice. The rice should always be bubbling slowly. If not, add some more stock. Continue adding the stock like this, until the rice is tender and creamy, but the grains remain firm, and the pumpkin is beginning to disintegrate. (This should take about 20 minutes, depending on the type of rice used.) Taste and season well with salt and pepper.

Stir the remaining butter and the Parmesan cheese into the rice. Cover and let the risotto rest for 2–3 minutes, then serve straight away with extra Parmesan cheese.

this **orange-coloured** risotto is a **rich** and **filling** meal-in-a-bowl just bursting with **fresh flavours**

There's something about the combination of seared fresh tuna and crisp, colourful Mediterranean vegetables tossed with a herby dressing that is very appealing. It's comforting in a fresh, clean sort of way. Cooking the tuna steaks on a griddle or a barbecue is also part of the pleasure – the aroma as they cook whets the appetite.

warm niçoise noodle salad
with seared tuna

serves 4

2 fresh tuna steaks, each weighing about 225g/8oz
175g/6oz fine green beans, trimmed
3 eggs
350g/12oz medium Chinese dried egg noodles
225g/8oz baby plum tomatoes, halved
50g/2oz can anchovy fillets, drained and fillets separated (optional)
50g/2oz/½ cup small black olives
a handful of fresh basil leaves, torn
salt and ground black pepper

For the marinade
30ml/2 tbsp lemon juice
75ml/5 tbsp olive oil
2 garlic cloves, crushed

For the warm dressing
90ml/6 tbsp extra virgin olive oil
30ml/2 tbsp wine vinegar or lemon juice
2 garlic cloves, crushed
2.5ml/½ tsp Dijon mustard
30ml/2 tbsp capers
45ml/3 tbsp chopped mixed herbs such as tarragon, chives, basil and chervil

To make the marinade, combine the lemon juice, olive oil and garlic in a glass or china dish. Add salt and pepper and mix well. Add the tuna and turn to coat in the marinade. Cover and leave to marinate in a cool place for 1 hour.

Whisk all the ingredients for the dressing together in a small pan and leave to infuse.

Meanwhile, blanch the green beans in boiling salted water for 4 minutes. Drain and refresh in cold water. In a separate pan, cover the eggs with plenty of cold water. Bring to the boil, then boil for 10 minutes. Immediately drain and cover with cold water to stop the cooking. When cool, shell and quarter the eggs.

Put the noodles and blanched beans into a bowl and pour boiling water over to cover. Leave for 5 minutes, then fork up the noodles. Heat the dressing and keep warm. Drain the noodles and beans, and toss with the dressing. Heat a ridged griddle pan or heavy skillet until smoking. Drain the tuna steaks, pat dry and sear for 1–2 minutes on each side. Remove and immediately slice thinly. Add the tuna with the halved tomatoes, anchovies and black olives to the noodles and beans, and toss well. Pile the salad into warmed serving bowls and scatter with the quartered eggs and basil. Season the salad well with salt and pepper and eat while it is still warm.

Home-cooked rice pudding is quite wonderful, especially when you lift the dark, crisp skin to reveal a sea of creamy caramel rice. If you really don't like the skin (shame!), simmer the pudding on top of the stove for about one hour instead of baking it.

caramel rice pudding
with apricot and almond compôte

serves 4

1 vanilla pod (bean), split
300ml/½ pint/1¼ cups milk
300ml/½ pint/1¼ cups evaporated milk
50g/2oz/¼ cup short grain pudding rice

For the caramel
115g/4oz/½ cup granulated sugar
90ml/6 tbsp water

For the compôte
75g/3oz/6 tbsp caster (superfine) sugar
225g/8oz/1 cup ready-to-eat dried apricots
50g/2oz/½ cup whole blanched almonds
a few drops bitter almond essence (extract), optional

Preheat the oven to 150°C/300°F/Gas 2. To make the caramel, put the sugar and half the water into a heavy pan. Leave over a low heat, without stirring, until the sugar has dissolved and the liquid is clear. Increase the heat and gently boil until the liquid turns a caramel colour. Remove the pan from the heat, stand back and add the remaining water – take care as it will hiss and splutter.

Return the pan to a low heat and stir to dissolve the hardened pieces of caramel. Take the caramel off the heat and leave to cool for 2 minutes.

To make the rice pudding, put the split vanilla pod, milk and evaporated milk into a pan and bring slowly to the boil. Stir in the rice and cooled caramel, bring back to the boil, then pour into a shallow 900ml/1½ pint/3¾ cup ovenproof dish.

Bake the pudding for about 3 hours or until a brown skin forms on top and the rice beneath is cooked and creamy.

Meanwhile, make the compôte. Put the caster sugar and 300ml/½ pint/1¼ cups water in a pan and heat until the sugar has dissolved. Add the apricots, then cover and simmer for 20 minutes until very soft. Stir in the almonds and essence, if using. Leave to cool, then chill.

Serve the rice pudding warm with the cooled apricot and almond compôte spooned on top.

the contrast between hot, **creamy** **caramel** rice and **chilled apricots** is something else indeed...

A fruit crumble cries out to be eaten on the sofa. It sits beautifully in a bowl, stays where it should – on the spoon and in the mouth – and willingly accepts lashings of cream. My first choice is for rhubarb, preferably the first of the season when it is bright pink and tender.

rhubarb and raspberry crumble

serves 4

675g/1½lb fresh forced rhubarb, cut into large chunks
a pinch of ground allspice
grated rind and juice of 1 lime
175g/6oz/scant 1 cup golden caster (superfine) sugar
225g/8oz fresh or frozen raspberries
custard or clotted cream, to serve

For the crumble
115g/4oz/1 cup plain (all-purpose) flour
pinch of salt
50g/2oz/½ cup ground almonds
115g/4oz/½ cup cold butter
115g/4oz/1 cup blanched almonds, chopped
50g/2oz/¼ cup golden caster (superfine) sugar

Preheat the oven to 200°C/400°F/Gas 6 and put a baking sheet inside to heat up. Put the rhubarb in a pan with the allspice, lime rind and juice and sugar. Cook over a gentle heat for 2 minutes, stirring occasionally, until the chunks of rhubarb are tender but still hold their shape.

Pour the rhubarb into a sieve, set over a bowl to catch the juices. Leave to cool. Reserve the juices for later.

To make the crumble, put the flour, pinch of salt, ground almonds and butter into a food processor and process until the mixture resembles fine breadcrumbs. Tip into a bowl and stir in the blanched almonds and sugar.

Spoon the rhubarb into a large ovenproof dish, and stir in the raspberries. Sprinkle the almond mixture evenly over the surface, mounding it up a little towards the centre.

Place the dish on the baking sheet in the oven and bake for 35 minutes until crisp and golden on top. Cool for 5 minutes before serving with custard or clotted cream and the warmed, reserved rhubarb juices.

the **pretty, pink** and slender rhubarb available at the beginning of the season has been grown in **pots by candlelight** – very romantic

This was the most wickedly indulgent dessert I could think of. You have the choice of making the ice cream, or just getting stuck into the rich brownies. I've been testing brownie recipes for years and reckon this is the best yet.

crumbled **chocolate brownie ice cream**

serves 6

1.2 litres/2 pints/5 cups good quality chocolate or chocolate chip ice cream

For the chocolate brownies
75g/3oz dark (bittersweet) chocolate with 70% cocoa solids
115g/4oz/½ cup butter, plus extra for greasing
4 eggs, beaten
10ml/2 tsp vanilla essence (extract)
400g/14oz/2 cups caster (superfine) sugar
115g/4oz/1 cup plain (all-purpose) flour
25g/1oz/¼ cup (unsweetened) cocoa powder
115g/4oz packet dark (bittersweet) chocolate chips
115g/4oz/1 cup chopped walnuts

First make the chocolate brownies. Preheat the oven to 190°C/375°F/Gas 5. Liberally butter an 18 x 28cm/7 x 11in shallow baking pan and line the base with baking parchment. Break up the chocolate into pieces and put it in a bowl with the butter. Place the bowl over a pan of barely simmering water and leave until the contents have melted. Remove the bowl from the heat and stir in the beaten eggs, vanilla and sugar. Mix well together.

Sift the flour with the cocoa powder and beat into the chocolate mixture. Gently stir in the chocolate chips and walnuts. Pour the mixture into the pan and level the surface. Bake for about 35 minutes. To test if the brownies are fully cooked, insert a metal skewer in the centre. The cake should be set but still moist. (Overcooking will make the brownies dry.) If you prefer a drier texture – which is better for the ice cream – cook for 10–15 minutes more. Leave the brownies to cool in the pan. When completely cold, cut into squares or bars.

To make the chocolate brownie ice cream, cut about 175g/6oz of the brownies into small cubes. Soften the ice cream and lightly stir in the chopped brownies. Spoon the mixture into a large freezerproof container, cover and freeze for at least 2 hours before serving.

mix leftover brownies into
vanilla ice cream and eat straight away
(this is true **late night stuff)**

back to bed

When it's cold and dark outside, there really is no other place to be but back in bed. The idea of taking something to eat or drink with you is immensely comforting; a last tasty morsel to encourage a sound sleep, perhaps, or a medicinal hot toddy to soothe the throat and still the sniffles (though don't think you have to wait for a cold before sipping this nightcap under the cover of the duvet). When it comes to eating at the end of the day, the basic requirements are few. Food and drink have to be rich, indulgent and utterly over the top.

Though difficult, I have managed to limit my choice to just two drinks and two dishes that really satisfy these terms. Of the drinks, my hot toddy is something of a speciality and, while others have their own favourite recipe, I've found that the combination of fresh lemons, fresh root ginger and whisky, with a spoonful of honey to sweeten, hits the spot every time.

at last, back to bed – the best place to be

My second choice for late night luxury in a glass is a hot buttered rum. It is said that this drink originated with the Pilgrim Fathers. Whether or not it was the beverage that gave them hope when times were hard is debatable, but it is certainly a miraculous drink. I made this once for my father, when he had been out in the pouring rain, trying to tie off our boat in a lock. He was soaked through, but the hot rum soon warmed him up as he sipped the milky drink through the thin layer of melted butter. The butter is such a extravagent extra — I love it. Try this drink if you really feel chilled to the bone. It is much better than a cup of cocoa and will raise your spirits as well as your temperature.

Bed is a place where you can be totally indulgent, so I've included two chocolate treats that are rich indeed. It's hard to fault chocolate when considering what food to take to bed with you – rich, luxurious, sublime; good quality chocolate is all these things. The first recipe is for a languorous chocolate mousse, which has the sensuous aftertaste of orange, achieved by combining the very best organic orange chocolate with Grand Marnier liqueur. The last recipe is for chocolate cookies sandwiched together with softly melting ice cream. This is a dish I find best eaten alone – it's hard to eat this with much decorum.

bedtime food should be simple, rich and
highly indulgent – this is the place to luxuriate
to your heart's content

Many of the recipes featured elsewhere in this book are also great for late-night cravings. A glass of warm and creamy egg nog, some rich, buttery shortbread, or a bacon sandwich to accompany the midnight movie, would not be out of place. Whatever you choose, the food and drink you have at bedtime should instantly appeal. It must be something you simply cannot go to sleep without consuming first. We know that hunger isn't what's prompting us here, but everyone needs a daily treat and, if you've missed out during the day, this is your very last chance.

Bed suggests warmth and comfort – a place where you can be safe and warm. Hot drinks are sheer luxury in bed, especially if you are feeling a little down or under the weather. A hot toddy is warming, soothing and has a lovely, almost fresh taste – the lemon, honey and whisky combine to take care of the most miserable cold. Hot buttered rum, on the other hand, is luxurious and pampering, especially when sipped through a layer of melted butter.

hot toddy

Put the lemon rind, ginger, honey and water in a small pan and bring to the boil. Remove from the heat and leave to infuse for 5 minutes. Stir the alcohol into the pan (despite the fact that I'm a Scot, my preference has always been for bourbon with its rounded, mellow, nutty taste), and allow time for it to warm through. Rest a silver spoon in warm glasses and strain in the warm toddy. Sip slowly.

serves 2

2 strips of pared lemon rind
4 slices of fresh root ginger
5ml/1 tsp honey
175ml/6fl oz/¾ cup water
175ml/6fl oz/¾ cup Scotch whisky, Irish whiskey or American bourbon

hot buttered rum

Heat the milk in a pan with the sugar and cinnamon stick. Pour in the rum and heat gently for 1–2 minutes.

Pour the mixture into warmed mugs and dot the surface with the butter. Grate nutmeg over the top. The top of each drink will soon be covered with a very thin layer of golden yellow melted butter, and sipping the hot, milky rum and nutmeg through this mixes the saltiness of the butter into the drink. This is one of my all-time favourite drinks.

serves 2

475ml/16fl oz/2 cups milk
15ml/1 tbsp caster (superfine) sugar
1 cinnamon stick
175ml/6fl oz/¾ cup dark navy rum
25g/1oz/2 tbsp unsalted butter, chopped into small pieces
freshly grated nutmeg

Everything about this mousse is seductive. The smooth, creamy chocolate lingers on the tongue after being slowly sucked off the spoon. Only the best chocolates have this effect, so save your most expensive, cocoa-solids-packed variety for this ultimate indulgence.

liqueur-spiked
chocolate orange mousse

Break the chocolate into pieces and put in a small bowl over a pan of barely simmering water. Pour in the liqueur and add the butter. Leave undisturbed for about 10 minutes until melted.

Separate the eggs and put the whites into a large mixing bowl with a tiny pinch of salt. Stir the chocolate mixture and remove from the heat. Quickly mix in the egg yolks.

Whisk the egg whites until stiff but not dry. Fold one large spoonful into the chocolate sauce to loosen the mixture, then carefully, but thoroughly, fold in the remaining egg whites.

Spoon the mixture into little pots or ramekins, cover and chill for at least 6 hours, or until set. Serve with thin strips of candied orange peel.

serves 4

200g/7oz orange-flavoured dark
(bittersweet) chocolate with more
than 60% cocoa solids
45ml/3 tbsp Grand Marnier liqueur
25g/1oz/2 tbsp unsalted butter
3 large (US extra large) eggs
salt
candied orange peel, to serve

a classic recipe that cannot be
equalled for its sheer sensuality

Take a pile of these to bed with you and all that will be left next morning will be the crumbs in the duvet. These are dangerous cookies. Crisp yet crumbly and packed with chocolate chips, they are a must with tall glasses of ice-cold milk or stacked with an obscene amount of ice cream.

late night **cookies**

**makes about 12 large or
20 small cookies**

75g/3oz/6 tbsp butter, softened
75g/3oz/6 tbsp golden caster
(superfine) sugar
75g/3oz soft light brown
sugar, sifted
1 large (US extra large) egg, beaten
2.5ml/½ tsp vanilla essence (extract)
150g/5oz/1¼ cups self-raising
(self-rising) flour
25g/1oz/¼ cup cocoa
powder (unsweetened)
1.5ml/¼ tsp salt
100g/4oz chopped chocolate or
plain (semisweet) chocolate chips
ice cream or milk, to serve

Preheat the oven to 180°C/350°F/Gas 4. Butter two heavy non-stick baking sheets. Cream the butter and sugars together until pale and fluffy. Beat in the egg and vanilla essence.

Sift the flour with the cocoa and salt. Gently fold into the egg mixture with the chopped chocolate or chocolate chips. Place four heaped tablespoonfuls of the mixture spaced well apart on each baking sheet. Press down and spread out with the back of a wet spoon. Bake the cookies in the oven for 12 minutes. Cool on the baking sheet for 1 minute, then remove to a cooling rack. Repeat with the remaining mixture. Store in an airtight container when cold. Serve with ice cream sandwiched between, or eat on their own with a glass of ice-cold milk.

how about a **darkly secretive** sandwich of chocolate chip **cookies** and **ice cream** at night – no one will see you

index

Author's acknowledgements

Many people have sat around my kitchen table over the years, offering love and knowledge. I would especially like to thank Jacks and Robert, Paul and Lyd, Laurie and Lesley, Annie-mate, Joyce and Jess K, who have all given or shared warmth, comfort, food (and butterballs) when I've most needed it.

Special thanks go to Martin Brigdale for always being able to get just that inspired shot, and for eating all those breakfasts. To Helen Trent for her creative and luscious styling, and to Linda Tubby, for making the food look just the way it should be – so natural, but still visually inviting – just the way I like it. They make a very special team.

Finally, many thanks to Margaret Malone and Linda Fraser for asking me to do this book, enthusing so much and still keeping me on schedule.

Publisher's acknowledgements

We would like to thank the following companies for the loan of material for photography:
Conran Shop: Michelin House, 81 Fulham Road,
London SW3 6RD. Tel: 020 7589 7401
Heals: 196 Tottenham Court Road, London W1T 7LQ.
Tel: 020 7636 1666
Purves and Purves: 220–224 Tottenham Court Road,
London W1T 7Q. Tel: 020 7636 1666